CHASING VINES

BETH MOORE

chasing vines

Finding your way to
an immensely fruitful life

TYNDALE
MOMENTUM®

The Tyndale nonfiction imprint

Visit Tyndale online at www.tyndale.com.

Visit Tyndale Momentum online at www.tyndalemomentum.com.

Visit Beth Moore online at www.lproof.org.

TYNDALE, Tyndale's quill logo, and *Tyndale Momentum* are registered trademarks of Tyndale House Publishers. The Tyndale Momentum logo is a trademark of Tyndale House Publishers. Tyndale Momentum is the nonfiction imprint of Tyndale House Publishers, Carol Stream, Illinois.

Chasing Vines: Finding Your Way to an Immensely Fruitful Life

Designed by Dean H. Renninger

Edited by Stephanie Rische

Published in association with Yates & Yates, LLP (yates2.com).

For information about special discounts for bulk purchases, please contact Tyndale House Publishers at csresponse@tyndale.com, or call 1-800-323-9400.

Library of Congress Cataloging-in-Publication Data
Names: Moore, Beth, date- author.
Title: Chasing vines : finding your way to an immensely fruitful life / Beth Moore.
Description: Carol Stream : Tyndale House Publishers, 2020. | Includes bibliographical references.
Identifiers: LCCN 2019027679 (print) | LCCN 2019027680 (ebook) | ISBN 9781496440822 (hardcover) |
     ISBN 9781496440846 (kindle edition) | ISBN 9781496440853 (epub) | ISBN 9781496440860 (epub)
Subjects: LCSH: Viticulture in the Bible. | Metaphor in the Bible. | Spiritual formation.
Classification: LCC BS665 .M66 2020 (print) | LCC BS665 (ebook) | DDC 248.4—dc23
LC record available at https://lccn.loc.gov/2019027679
LC ebook record available at https://lccn.loc.gov/2019027680

ISBN 978-1-4964-4479-0 (ITPE)

Printed in the United States of America

26   25   24   23   22   21   20
7   6   5   4   3   2   1

To Amanda and Melissa,
my beloved daughters,
my very heart,
my best friends,
my favorite fellow sojourners—
because of Italy.

CONTENTS

INTRODUCTION

Here's what I know after decades of life and ministry among myriads of people: *we all want to matter.* The yearning to matter is no respecter of persons. Man or woman; adult or child; religious or irreligious; rich or poor; black, brown, or white—such a longing is sewn in permanent thread within the fabric of every human soul.

The great relief is finding out that the hope is not deferred. You do matter—already—without making one single change. But everything changes when you let your Maker show you why you matter and how He can take all that concerns you and, sooner or later, here or there, subtly or astonishingly, make it matter.

We were created to contribute, fashioned to bring who we are and what we have to the human mix to add some measure of benefit. This was true even in Eden's unmarred paradise. God said to Adam and Eve, in so many words, *Add to it! Work the ground! And the two of you, be fruitful and multiply. Fill the earth!*

Jesus elevated the concept to another stratosphere by taking individuals He'd given abundant life to and, by the power of His own Spirit, making their contributions matter not just temporally, as He did with Adam and Eve, but eternally.

> *By this my Father is glorified, that you bear much fruit and*
> *so prove to be my disciples. . . . You did not choose me, but*
> *I chose you and appointed you that you should go and bear*
> *fruit and that your fruit should abide.*
> JOHN 15:8, 16

This idea that our lives matter has been tailing me for as long as I can remember, but now, as I get closer and closer to the finish line, the concept practically haunts me. When I get to the end of my life, I want to know that it meant something. I want to know that my life, in all its fits and starts, mattered.

If you feel the same, it's not just us—God wants our lives to matter too. He means for us to be profoundly effective. That longing in us to contribute, to do something worthwhile, isn't just a self-consumed dream. If we follow Jesus, that's what we can hope to expect from life.

And being fruitful isn't some stale and banal duty. It directly affects how happy we are, because engaging in what God is doing is the only thing that gives us true satisfaction and peace. God is invading the globe with the gospel of Christ, pursuing people from every tongue, tribe, and nation, offering them life, faith, love, hope, deliverance, joy, and a forever future where He reigns as King. Nothing happening on earth is more meaningful or exhilarating. And as we bear much fruit, we get to be part of it.

I know what it's like to fear not being seen. I know what it's like to worry that I'm not of use. I know how easy it is to feel giftless in a gift-driven society. If you're anything like me, you long to contribute. You long to matter. And you know what? You do.

You don't have to settle for just making it. In Christ, you can make it matter.

✦ ✦ ✦

I have been enamored with Christ's teaching on the vine and the branches since I cut my teeth on Bible study, and I've taught about His call to fruitfulness as an essential part of life's satisfaction for at least twenty years. The spectacular thing about Scripture, however, is that, like no other book held in human hands, its ink may be dry but it is the furthest thing from dead. The words are alive and active, and the Holy Spirit who inspired them can animate the most familiar passage and spring it to fresh life in your soul.

It happened to me in Tuscany a year ago, on a dream trip I took with my daughters, Amanda and Melissa. Beyond the self-centered joy of being with the two of them, my hope for this trip that we'd been planning for ages was to reward them. They didn't ask for the mother they got. By the time my daughters were four and one, I was away virtually every other Friday night—usually just for one night, and their daddy took charge. A few nights a month may not sound like a lot at first blush, but no little girl wants her mommy to leave. Forty years of ministry exacts a toll on a family. Yet my three main people, Keith, Amanda, and Melissa, have somehow managed to resist the woeful punishment of seething resentment. I am blessed beyond expression, inconceivably graced, and pray that God will return it to them in eternal rewards.

But since we aren't in heaven yet, I thought maybe He wouldn't mind getting a jump on it and blessing them with something temporal that I got to be in on before I was so old I couldn't tell the girls apart. I had in mind something that would almost certainly be useless to the Kingdom except for building up the souls of three Jesus-serving women with good coffee, good food, good conversation, and if laughter is good medicine (and the Bible says it is), enough good laughter to anesthetize a battalion. The Lord didn't seem to object.

I was determined to pay for three round-trip tickets to Italy with frequent flyer miles, not only because I'm cheap, but also for the pure symbolism of returning a deposit to them for all the times I'd boarded an airplane to who-knows-where. It took nearly every mile I'd stashed, but each one was worth it.

Seven hours later, we landed in Florence, the famed cradle of the Renaissance, where we added twenty miles of calluses to the soles of our feet before waving a sad goodbye to Michelangelo's *David*. By the time we boarded a flight back to the States, we had toured Siena, hit up Naples, drove the Amalfi Coast, and stayed several nights in Positano, the iconic spot we'd been promised would be our all-time favorite. We took a motorboat to lunch, rode a ferry to Capri, and spent our final nights in Sorrento. The adventure certainly qualified for a trip of a lifetime—everything we three American women wanted it to be and more. But none of those stops were the scene of my unexpected romance.

My undoing was rural Tuscany. The place was otherworldly. We stayed three nights at an inn twenty minutes from Siena, light years from our lives in Houston. The inn was built on a hillside in the upper quadrant of a vineyard, overlooking other hills that rolled in crestless waves into the horizon. I could stand on the grounds and turn around and around, and every direction I looked, I saw vines.

We weren't savvy enough to time our stay in Tuscany at the tail end of the harvest, or we'd have been insufferably proud of ourselves. Instead, it was an incontrovertible gift of grace to us

WHEN I GET
TO THE END OF
MY LIFE, I WANT
TO KNOW THAT IT
meant
SOMETHING.

neophytes—an unexpected present from God wrapped in ribbons of green, violet, brown, and gold. The only thing we had going for us is that the gift was not wasted on us.

On our way into town by taxi one Tuscan morning, winding through her undulating hills, we saw the last of the harvesters walking the rows—inspecting the vines and clipping the final heavy clusters of fruit. Captivated, I felt like I was watching live reenactments of some of Christ's own parables (Matthew 20, 21). It was not lost on me that one of His final exhortations to His disciples was, essentially, "Be immensely fruitful" (John 15:5-8).

The trip was just supposed to be a sightseeing vacation, not a Bible study tour, but I couldn't help myself. I figured if Jesus spent so much time talking about vines, the closer I got to them, the more I stood to learn. If I was going to understand what it means to follow Jesus, I couldn't skim over this or chalk it up to an extinct cultural phenomenon, gone the way of head coverings and purification rituals. I needed to follow this undeniable tug on my heart.

And that's where I fell in love, my nose pressed to the window of the taxi, my palms on the glass, like someone trying to escape a carload of kidnappers. That was the beginning of my grape crush. It was Giuseppe Verdi who famously said, "You may have the universe if I may have Italy." Ah, and you, Giuseppe, may have Italy if I may have her vines.

The image of the vineyard has consumed me ever since that trip, instigating a chase from cover to cover in the sacred pages, to shelves of commentaries and dictionaries. It has sent me into hours of interviews with experts on everything from planting vines to processing grapes into wines, and into a stack of books halfway to the ceiling on the same. With every piece of research, my fascination with vine and branch imagery has grown. God put the song of the vineyard on my phonograph, set the stylus to vinyl, turned up the volume, and swept me off my feet.

Perhaps you know how the parable goes: sometimes you find a hidden treasure, and in your uncontainable joy, you save up, go back, and buy the whole field (Matthew 13:44). I found a cluster of grapes on a gorgeous vine and couldn't stop myself until I'd dug up the field.

And I don't want to keep the treasure I found in Italy to myself. I want to share it with you. There's a taxi waiting with an open seat. I'll scoot over if you'll climb in, and if you're willing to put your heart into it, you might just fall in love too.

+ + +

In her poem "The Summer Day," Mary Oliver asks an unforgettable question deeply worth pondering:

Tell me, what is it you plan to do
with your one wild and precious life?

That wild and precious life of yours matters—to God and to the world. Not a drop of it is wasted.

Your work matters.
Your gifts matter.
Your tears matter.
Your pain matters.
Your joy matters.
Your hopes matter.
Your dreams matter.
Your successes matter.

Your failures matter.

Your relationships matter.

Your memories matter.

Your childhood matters.

Your past matters.

Your future matters.

Your present matters.

God uses it—all of it. In the hands of the Vinedresser, nothing is dropped. Everything matters.

God wants you to flourish in Him. Every last thing He plants in your life is intended for that purpose. If we give ourselves fully to His faithful ways, mysterious and painful though they may be at times, we will find that it's all part of the process that enables us to grow and bear fruit. Those Tuscan vines will have nothing on us.

And so we find ourselves at a crossroads. If we have guts enough to believe that we were created by God to flourish in Christ, we have a choice to make. Will we sit idly by and wait for it to happen, as if our cooperation isn't part of the process? Or will we set out, light on our feet, with hearts ablaze, and give chase to this call to flourish?

Amid all the vine-chasing we have ahead in these pages, here's the best part: I think we'll find that, all along, the Vine Himself has been chasing us. "Your beauty and love chase after me every day of my life" (Psalm 23:6, MSG).

The grapes are ripe. The vineyard awaits. Come, join me in the chase.

PART 1

The Vineyard

The LORD God
planted a garden.

GENESIS 2:8

CHAPTER 1

plant

Eight years ago, in a fit of urban angst, Keith and I pulled up stakes and moved to the country. I'd said I'd never leave that city house. I'd sworn he'd have to bury my cold, stiff body in the backyard, where the bones of our family pets rested in as much peace as our new puppies would allow them. I'd raised two little girls there. They'd driven their Big Wheels up and down that driveway, then their bikes. They'd pulled out of that same driveway, cars bulging with suitcases, towels, and brand-new bedspreads when they'd driven off to college.

But inch by inch, the city had tried to smother us. Every field where we'd walked our dogs, held hands again after quarrels, and cleared our clogged-up lungs of odorous air had been strategically buried under concrete. By the time the fourth storage unit went up within a four-block radius, we were howling at the moon.

We took Keith's parents with us. They lived within a minute

of our front door and had moved to our subdivision so we could share life with them and care for them. We couldn't move without them, and we had no idea if they had the energy—emotional or physical, either one—to pick up and put down all over again. We decided to pop the question over taco salads at their house later that week. "Here's what we're thinking. Would you help us find a sliver of woods and go with . . . ?" They were in the car before we were.

That move changed a lot of things for us. Our pace of life slowed, we exchanged the sound of traffic for a nightly chorus of frogs and crickets, and my commute to work went from freeways to two-lane roads, only some of them paved. But perhaps the most surreal change of all stemmed from the plot of land we dug up to make our own vegetable garden.

Once you spend time digging around in your own little patch of dirt and tasting the fruit of your labors, it's hard to eat a tomato the same way again.

And since God is the ultimate Gardener, I have to believe He feels the same way.

✝   ✝   ✝

"In the beginning."

Creation brought out the earthy side of heaven. On the third day, God created dirt and liked it. In light of His all-knowingness, perhaps we should be more Presbyterian about the matter and say that He liked dirt, so He created it. It is a poor soul who confuses dirt with filth or soil with soiled.

Dirt drapes this spinning rock we call earth with a fine epidermis—pocked, porous, and thirsty. Dirt accommodates ants with both heap and hole. It memorializes every creature afoot, lizard and leopard alike, with at least a fleeting footprint. The dirt under an elephant's toenails may end up as sunscreen for his delicate hide when he tosses it by trunk onto his back.

The fact is, in the hands of the consummate Potter, dirt is raw material for His wheel.

When no bush of the field was yet in the land and no small plant of the field had yet sprung up—for the LORD God had not caused it to rain on the land, and there was no man to work the ground, and a mist was going up from the land and was watering the whole face of the ground . . .
GENESIS 2:5-6

The writer appears to make a point of the sequence of events. There was land but no bush or plant of any kind. No holly, jasmine, or juniper. No hyssop for painting doorposts red. No hydrangea for vases on tables full of bread. And there were no humans to miss them. There was only mist—rain in strange reverse. It came from the underside of the earth, wet enough to dampen the dust if someone wanted to make a mud pie.

The LORD God formed the man of dust from the ground and breathed into his nostrils the breath of life, and the man became a living creature. And the LORD God planted a garden in Eden, in the east, and there he put the man whom he had formed.
GENESIS 2:7-8

After bringing the universe into being by nothing but His voice, God thrust His hands downward into the soil (*adamah* in

GOD LIKES
WATCHING
THINGS

grow.

Hebrew) and fashioned a human (*adam*). Both man and the patch of ground that God ordained to busy and sustain him were the stuff of divine touch. Direct contact.

The English word *human* literally means "a creature of earth," from the word *humus*, or ground.[1] The humble word *humble* comes from the same origin and means "lowly, near the ground."[2] God appointed gravity to keep us there.

The idea of God at arm's length is a comfortable thought, particularly since the Almighty Himself claimed His arms were not short. We could imagine the Creator with arms long enough to keep His face from getting dusty through the whole creative ordeal, but blowing breath into the human's nostrils sketches a different posture.

Here we have a Maker leaning low, near to the ground. Here we have God who is high and lifted up but is now bending over, animating dust. God, mouth-to-nose with man.

+ + +

Right about now you might be wondering why, in a book about vines and vineyards, I've gone all the way back—literally, to the beginning. My grandmother Minnie Ola Rountree used to say I was one of those people who would recount the invention of the sundial if you asked me what time it was.

I admit it. I am obsessed with origins. I'm also convinced to my bones, and cheerfully so, that most people find origins fascinating, once they see the connections. Before we can mine the riches of vines and grapes, we need some context. We need to set the scene for the vineyard—we need to get down on our knees and dig around in the soil a bit to find out why the process of growing things is important to God, and therefore why it's important to us.

The LORD God planted a garden in Eden.
GENESIS 2:8

The reason planting is so crucial to appreciating the process is because it is spectacularly deliberate. In life, so many unexplainable things happen that can make a person feel like everything is one enormous accident. Some dots never do seem to connect. Your present job may appear to have nothing to do with your last job. You may feel like what you were trained to do has no link to what you're actually doing.

We long for continuity, for some semblance of purpose—anything that might suggest we're on the right track. Instead, we feel like ashes, leftovers from a bygone fire, blown aimlessly by the wind. We feel like we're not even important enough to be forgotten, because we were never known in the first place.

Our perceptions can be very convincing, but God tells us the truth. Nothing about our existence is accidental. We were known before we knew we were alive. We were planned and, as a matter of fact, *planted* on this earth for this moment in time (Acts 17:26).

When Jesus told His disciples, "My Father is the gardener" (John 15:1, NLT), He wasn't using random imagery to sketch His point. Jesus' Father had waited no longer than Genesis 2:8 to go on record that He is a home gardener. Goodness knows, He could have afforded to contract it out, but we get no glimpse of angelic landscapers.

For those who have a whiff of imagination, the scene here is God Himself with hoe and spade. It's God who's afoot with herbs and bulbs. It's God with the knack and no *Farmers' Almanac.* In our corner of the world, where most flowerpots are screenshots, it's grounding to remember that humankind's first culture was horticulture. Every time we use the word *culture*, we're talking gardening. In Latin, *cultura* means a cultivated land.

The Bible uses gardening terms for the acts of God time and again. In 2 Samuel 7:10, God is described as appointing a people and not placing them, but rather planting them where He wanted them. Psalm 94:9 says God planted the ear on man, and according to Luke 22:51, Jesus could also clearly replant one, should that be necessary. Words like *rooted* and *uprooted* and *grounded* all speak the language of horticulture.

> *Out of the ground the LORD God made to spring up every tree that is pleasant to the sight and good for food.*
> GENESIS 2:9

God made to spring up. It's a wonder that God would choose to slowly grow what He could have simply created grown. Why on earth would He go to the trouble to plant a garden forced to sprout rather than commanding it into existence, full bloom? Why leave His desk and get His pant legs soiled?

Because God likes watching things grow.

✦   ✦   ✦

Several years passed from the time we hatched our dream of moving to the country until the moving vans pulled up to our curb. We spent countless evenings driving the outskirts of Houston in search of a small chorus of trees whispering "Welcome home" to four city-weary warriors. We finally found them down a long dirt road that was only one car's width.

To preoccupy ourselves through the drawling, hair-pulling, haggling months of home building, we had a rectangle of land ploughed up for a vegetable garden. All spring long, we made the drive out to those woods on dirt roads so rock pocked it sounded like our tires were driving over Bubble Wrap.

Once we reached our destination, our only amenities were four rusty lawn chairs we'd leave leaned up against a pine tree. We'd unfold them, their stiff joints screeching, and brush pine needles and spiderwebs off the seats. As long as the bird droppings were dry, we'd just go ahead and sit on them. Country living demanded a certain heartiness, after all.

We watered those mounds, walked the rows, steadied the stakes, and pulled up the weeds. But most of the time we just sat in those four lawn chairs and stared that garden down, willing our little plants to grow. And lo and behold, they did. Even a fallen Eden recollects how to delight fallen humans. Our tomato plants were a little on the leggy side, but the stems were spry and sinewy. Every tiny orb was love at first sight.

"We grow our own food," we'd say over and over while we sat in our lawn chairs gnawing our drive-thru Kentucky Fried Chicken down to the bones.

When our melons were no larger than boiled eggs, we swore we'd enter them in a contest and win. We railed about pests gnawing our squash. We used words like *blight* and *nymph* and *hornworm* like we knew what they meant. Keith and his dad turned into ten-year-old boys, cussing and spitting and poorly digesting. His mom and I clawed at mosquito bites and wished for verve enough to squat behind the bushes. It was the best of times.

I was neck deep in commentaries, studying a Bible lesson, when I got the call at work. "We have a ripe tomato."

Before the sun could set on that beginner's paradise, we farming posers were sitting foursquare in our lawn chairs, Big Pops holding up a tomato no bigger than a five-year-old's fist, like Rafiki holding up Simba. He drew his pearl-handle pocketknife from his faded overalls with ceremonial slowness and slid the short, stained blade through the meat twice to quarter it. Juice dripped merrily into his palm. There was no rinsing. No salting. No adding to. No taking away.

Grinning from ear-to-ear, with tomato pulp atop our chins and seeds between our teeth, we waved our firstfruits before God with gleeful hearts and received it the way the earth offered it.

Have you ever wondered why God goes to the trouble of sanctifying us? He could instantly zap us into His image the moment we decide to follow Jesus, or He could transport us into heaven the moment of our conversion. Why would He opt for taking us through the long, drawn-out process of planting, watering, pruning, and harvesting? But sure enough, He rolls up His sleeves, puts palms to the dirt, and begins putting the pieces of our lives together in a way that matters.

I think it's because He's not looking for a store-bought tomato. He wants the real thing, raised by His own hands, hard won as it is.

To a gardener, grown is overrated. It's growing it that makes the fruit sweet.

CHAPTER 2

place

Over the years, I've had the hardest time figuring out where I belong. I'll think, *This is it!* and the next thing I know, that hostile dog of insecurity starts nipping at my heels again, telling me I'm out of place. I'm either not enough or too much almost everywhere I go.

Do you ever get that same feeling? I'm forever searching for a place that fits me like a glove. "I'm a mountain girl," I'll claim. God knows I love the mountains, but it's not like I want to camp in them. Give me a day hike and then a hot bath and a hearty supper in a hotel room. "What I really am is an ocean girl." But then again, how committed to the beach can you be in a pair of shorts? The thing is, I have this paranoia about opening social media and seeing my aged white legs in a swimsuit. "I'm a cold-weather girl," I'll say—until I'm in Chicago for a couple of icy days in March, while the bluebonnets are blooming in Houston. Good grief, I don't know what kind of girl I am.

I've gone through this search for the perfect fit on a denominational level, too. "Maybe what I am is a Methodist. Or a Pentecostal. Maybe that's where I belong." I once asked my professor friend Cheryl to explain to me what a Wesleyan was to see if I was one of those. After countless conversations, I've come to the conclusion that what most of us have in common is the feeling that we're misfits.

I've also been told a few times to stay in my place. I wanted to respond, "I'd be more than happy to, if I could just figure out where on earth my place is."

Maybe nothing is more normal than feeling a bit abnormal. Maybe feeling comfortable in our own skin means coming to the realization that we weren't created to feel particularly comfortable in this skin.

This chapter is for all of us looking for our place, because after all, what's a plant without a place?

✛   ✛   ✛

For the past twelve months, I've been on this adventure in viticulture—the culture and cultivation of grapes. As we dig into Scripture in the pages of this book, we're gleaning insights into the divine makings of an immensely fruitful life. To achieve that goal, we have to set the vine free in the hand of the Gardener.

The Bible is a large book, and the grape, its favorite fruit. No single metaphor, symbol, or interpretation carries through from Genesis to Revelation. Our job is not to force the grape to go where we want it to go; ours is to go with the grape where it takes us.

I urge you to whet your taste for poetic imagery, lest these pages offer merely a ceramic bowl of table grapes, while the wine is missed altogether. It would be a crying shame for you to reach the end of this book with all raisins and no romance, all skins and no pulp. Even the natural science of viticulture drips with the romance of the vine.

The art and science of grape growing add sublime minerals to the soil of the vine in Scripture. After all, they find their origins in the inscrutable mind of God. I think one of the loveliest terms in viticulture is *terroir* (pronounced "ter-war") meaning "sense of place."[1] You can see its relationship to the word *terre*, meaning "earth," but terroir encompasses more than ground. It captures the interplay between factors such as soil, climate, the plant itself, and its orientation toward the sun. Together, these factors ultimately shape the "personality" of the resulting fruit.[2]

In this book, our primary terroir, or sense of place, is John 15, where Christ identifies His Father as the Vinedresser, Himself as the Vine, and His followers as the branches. It's the preeminent chapter on biblical viticulture.

Although Jesus is preeminent in all things, we can't stuff Him in every grape leaf in Scripture. He doesn't want to fit. He *won't* fit. That said, we will end up missing the revolutionary nature of His fulfillment of the Vine in John 15 if we don't appreciate the metaphor's other meanings elsewhere.

In the Bible, the vineyard sometimes represents prosperity, or the lack of it—the ravages of captivity. Sometimes the vine represents a woman, even a lover. Sometimes it represents a mother, fruitful in childbearing. Sometimes a vineyard represents the people of God.

Other times a singular vine represents Israel. Such is the case in the imagery that will preoccupy us in this chapter.

We find this metaphor in the very center of Psalm 80, a wailing song of Asaph.

Restore us, O God of hosts;
let your face shine, that we may be saved!

You brought a vine out of Egypt;
you drove out the nations and planted it.
You cleared the ground for it;
it took deep root and filled the land.
The mountains were covered with its shade,
the mighty cedars with its branches.
It sent out its branches to the sea
and its shoots to the River.
Why then have you broken down its walls,
so that all who pass along the way pluck its fruit?
The boar from the forest ravages it,
and all that move in the field feed on it.

Turn again, O God of hosts!
Look down from heaven, and see;
have regard for this vine,
the stock that your right hand planted,
and for the son whom you made strong for yourself.

PSALM 80:7-15

I love how the psalmist didn't mind reminding God who His people were to Him. The best part is that this approach was God's idea in the first place. By placing these lyrics on the permanent page, God was reminding His people to remind Him.

Of course, He could never forget, but out of the bounty of His mercy, He gifted worshipers with the language to recount His commitment to them and to call upon His faithfulness to act on that commitment.

There's nothing irreverent about an earnest worshiper crying out, "O God, have regard for Your people and for the place where You planted us!" Matters of people and place mark the Bible from cover to cover.

In the natural science of viticulture, these are the first two steps in planting a vineyard:

1. selecting the grape variety
2. choosing a vineyard site[3]

So I'm curious. Did God, the Vinedresser, follow the same order? In other words, which came first: the people or the place?

In the Old Testament, God's selection of His people, whom He would later reference as both the vine and the vineyard, took place in Genesis 12:1: "The LORD said to Abram, 'Go from your country and your kindred and your father's house to the land that I will show you.'"

At first blush, this could be taken to mean that the place takes precedence over the person. "Go . . . to the land." It may seem that God set aside the land and then called the man. But Isaiah 45:18 declares what multiple passages echo: God created the earth deliberately for the purpose of inhabiting it with humans.

Thus says the LORD, who created the heavens (he is God!),
who formed the earth and made it (he established it; he did
not create it empty, he formed it to be inhabited!).

The crown of God's creation was *image bearers*. This whirling rock, numbered third from the sun, was uniquely designed for hospitality toward humankind.

Therefore, we might rightly say that viticulture's most common steps for preparing a vineyard were ordered by the Lord: first the selection of the variety of grape, then the selection of a place to plant it.

Said another way,

first, the people,
then the place
for the people.

I was a young adolescent when the hit "Love the One You're With" was getting perpetual airplay. My friends and I quoted the lyrics to that song for years and teased one another for living by them. We even used these words as an excuse to dance with other guys at a party if our boyfriends weren't there. But later, all alone in the dark of night, surely I wasn't the only one who worried about being chosen simply because I was in arm's reach.

The lyrics were mainly just a clever play on words, but how many of us have felt that way . . . like someone picked us merely because we were convenient, and then when things got difficult, they moved on to someone else?

My point is, humans are a bit more inclined to choose the place first, then the person.

That's not the way God works. He didn't choose you because you happened to be in the right place at the right time or because nobody better was in arm's reach. God's arm is neither short nor weak (Isaiah 59:1). No one is out of His reach. If He chose you, He did so on purpose. Ephesians 1:4 declares with spectacular clarity, "He chose us in [Christ] before the foundation of the world."

And believe this: if you've been chosen by God, there is no room for equivocation: *you matter.*

+ + +

Once God made known who His people would be, He revealed where they would grow and flourish. The point about terroir is significant in Israel's history, because the vine (in the present metaphor, Abraham's descendants) faced a fair amount of uprooting and replanting.

For all its preoccupation with terroir, Israel had a fierce struggle with actual occupation throughout the Bible. In the days of the patriarchs, the vine took tentative root, but by the end of Genesis, it was pulled from its impotent, famine-starved ground and transplanted in the Nile-infused soil of Egypt. Rather than wither up and die, however, Israel prospered wildly—first under the favor of pharaohs familiar with Joseph, Abraham's great-grandson, and then under a pharaoh who zealously sought the Israelites' harm.

According to Exodus 1:5, a total of seventy descendants were originally transplanted into Egypt.

> *The people of Israel were fruitful and increased greatly; they multiplied and grew exceedingly strong, so that the land was filled with them.*
> EXODUS 1:7

In ancient Egypt, just as it is today, prejudice was fueled by fear, and the new pharaoh had no shortage of fuel. The people of Israel became so many and so mighty that he was enveloped by a paranoia of mutiny. He commanded his people to work the Israelites ruthlessly and afflict them until they complied.

The more they were oppressed, the more they multiplied and the more they spread abroad. And the Egyptians were in dread of the people of Israel.

EXODUS 1:12

So the pharaoh did what any maniacal dictator would do. He concocted a plan to eliminate a sizable chunk of the population he hated. He ordered the Egyptian midwives to slaughter at birth every baby boy of the Hebrew people. Fearing God above Pharaoh, the midwives let them live, claiming the mothers were so hearty, their babies were born before a nurse could arrive.

Frustrated, he came up with a second plan, but this time, he didn't limit the job to deficient midwives. This time he spread his indoctrination of elimination to the entire Egyptian population: "Cast all the Hebrew baby boys into the swollen Nile!" (Exodus 1:22).

One such baby boy, a beauty to his parents, as babes are wont to be, was swaddled by his mother's trembling hands and tucked inside a tiny ark made of bulrushes and waterproofed with pitch, then placed among the reeds at the river's edge, where Pharaoh's daughter bathed. The mother hid, the baby cried, and the stranger had pity.

Moses. The name means "drawn out of the water."

Then, eighty years and untold tears and fears later, here's the scene:

The people of Israel groaned because of their slavery and cried out for help. Their cry for rescue from slavery came up to God. And God heard their groaning, and God remembered his covenant with Abraham, with Isaac, and with Jacob. God saw the people of Israel—and God knew.

EXODUS 2:23-25

Three words: *and God knew.* He always does. But what exactly did it mean that He knew? That He loved them? That they belonged to Him? But hadn't that always been true?

All that God knows, He has always known. Does that mean He simply knew it was time? That they'd borne the burden long enough? That He'd heard them wailing quite long enough?

Decades earlier, Moses had taken the law into his own hands by killing an Egyptian for beating a Hebrew. Now the Lord found Moses on the backside of the desert, having flown from Pharaoh. And God sent the man drawn from the Nile back to the Nile to lead His people away from the Nile.

Now hear the line from the lamenting lyrics of Asaph:

You transplanted a vine from Egypt.
PSALM 80:8, NIV

This psalm was written centuries after the Moses saga, but the people of God were again in dire need of deliverance, as they were captives far from home. The lyrics give them voice to say to their God, essentially, "Do it again!"

And God knew. God knew that slavery wasn't the end of His people's story. He knew the enemy wouldn't get the final victory. He knew He would keep His promises in dramatic fashion. He had delivered them before, and He would deliver them again. The same is true for you, whether you're battling a vicious ruler or a vicious disease, whether you're up against an occupying army or your own anxiety.

God transplanted the vine—He snatched it right out of the ground and carried it out of Egypt, with four centuries of roots dangling, so He could plant it back in the soil of its belonging. Its home. Its true terroir.

It's no random stroke of the pen that Psalm 80 begins with a reference to Joseph: "Give ear, O Shepherd of Israel, you who lead Joseph like a flock."

The mention of Joseph is of prime importance, as the psalm shifts quickly from a shepherd-flock motif to include a parable of the vine. The patriarch Jacob (whom God renamed Israel) spoke prophetic blessings over each of his sons just prior to his death. These blessings applied not only to the individual specified by name but also to the tribe that would descend from him.

Keep in mind that Jacob's entire family, seventy in number, was in Egypt at the time these declarations were spoken. They had been reunited on what to them was completely foreign soil. The destruction the older sons intended when they sold their little brother Joseph into slavery had been overtaken by God for good. From the long view over his shoulder, Joseph recognized that God Himself had sent him ahead of the family to preserve their lives during a famine.

After blessing and prophesying over ten of his twelve sons, Jacob turned his eyes to the eleventh, his beloved Joseph, and unleashed words with significant imagery:

> *Joseph is a fruitful vine, a fruitful vine near a spring, whose branches climb over a wall.*
>
> GENESIS 49:22, NIV

Mind you, what Joseph had endured was still fresh on his mind. The seventy had only recently been reunited. Family wounds had barely begun to heal. But the fact was, while the rest of the family had been starving back in their homeland, first by famine of soul and then by famine of body, Joseph, the one who had been wronged, was inexplicably fruitful.

True belonging
IS FOUND ONLY IN
THE SOVEREIGN
PALM OF GOD.

Had the process been long and painful? Yes. Had his brothers done him wrong? Yes. Did they bear responsibility? Yes. Had God redeemed his slavery for good? Yes.

Was the pain ultimately worth it to Joseph?

Perhaps he considered this question as he shifted his gaze from over his shoulder to the sight in front of him. He would have seen old and young alike. He would have seen men, women, and children. He would have heard chatter, perhaps laughter and singing.

As Joseph stared at the faces of family members who had been spared, was the length and depth of his pain worth it? Undoubtedly, yes. God had transplanted the vine into Egypt for survival, and then, when the time was right, He would pluck it out of Egypt to replant it in its homeland.

That process would not go particularly smoothly either, but God is nothing if not patient. Israel would go to Canaan, and her ramparts would rise around Jerusalem. They'd also collapse one day, and the roots of the vine would whip in the wind again.

But for now, let's return to Psalm 80 and note the names that follow the mention of Joseph.

Give ear, O Shepherd of Israel,
*   you who lead Joseph like a flock.*
You who are enthroned upon the cherubim, shine forth.
*   Before Ephraim and Benjamin and Manasseh,*
stir up your might
*   and come to save us!*
PSALM 80:1-2

I want to draw special attention to the name Ephraim here—Joseph's younger son. Joseph gave both his sons meaningful names, but Ephraim is the one with deep purple relevance in the cultivation of God's choice vine.

> *The name of the second [Joseph] called Ephraim, "For God has made me fruitful in the land of my affliction."*
> GENESIS 41:52

Not *before* the land of his affliction. Not *after* the land of his affliction. In the smack-*middle* of the land of his affliction. Never confuse fruitfulness with felicity. That's not to say that fruit bearing can't be fun. But equate the two—fruitfulness and fun—and you'll miss some of your most fertile opportunities to bear inexplicable fruit. Sometimes the Nile will serve you better than the Jordan.

✝ ✝ ✝

Nothing can get more confusing than feeling planted somewhere you're sure is home and then getting uprooted and transplanted somewhere else. Without warning, you face the prospect of having to start all over again. You had your terroir. Your sense of place. You thought you knew how this was going to go. Your future seemed clear. Your people were near. And now you feel like a stranger in a foreign land.

Sometimes you'll stay in that unfamiliar land for longer than you ever imagined. Other times God will pluck you up and move you right back to your homeland, only for you to come to the bewildering reality that, although the place hasn't changed, you have.

We live our lives looking for home. We crave a sense of place. We are roots dangling in the air, carried by the wind, looking frantically for fitting terroir.

But that's part of the mystery. Part of the romance, really. For here and now, our terroir cannot be found in any plot of terrestrial ground.

Joseph and Mary knew the feeling. Their home was Nazareth. Their people were there. Their synagogue was there. But then a census took them on an arduous journey to Bethlehem, Joseph's ancestral home, where Mary gave birth to the son not of Joseph, her betrothed, but of God Most High.

The couple tarried there until wise men from the east, who were searching for the one born King of the Jews, had time to find Him and offer Him gifts and homage. All the while, surely the young couple had every expectation of returning home to their native soil. Then, while they were still in Bethlehem, the vine was uprooted to a most interesting place.

> When [the wise men] had departed, behold, an angel of the Lord appeared to Joseph in a dream and said, "Rise, take the child and his mother, and flee to Egypt, and remain there until I tell you, for Herod is about to search for the child, to destroy him." And he rose and took the child and his mother by night and departed to Egypt and remained there until the death of Herod. This was to fulfill what the Lord had spoken by the prophet, "Out of Egypt I called my son."
>
> MATTHEW 2:13-15

After Herod died, God plucked Joseph, Mary, and Jesus up again and planted them back in their familiar Nazarene soil.

"You transplanted a vine from Egypt," the psalmist sang.

Well, in this case, it wasn't just a vine. It would turn out to be *the* Vine. Interestingly, that Vine never really found its native soil here.

There are some mysteries in viticulture that can't be fully satisfied scientifically. They are simply meant to be appreciated. Among them is terroir. The finest vinedressers in Tuscany could plant a vine in a perfect spot, but they can't make the soil comply. They could choose the right climate, but they can't control the weather. They could strive for consistency in water and fertilizer, but they can't force the vine to produce the same wine produced by its neighbor tied to the next trellis. The mysteries of terroir can be studied, but they can't all be solved.

So with us. Nothing haunts us more than our search for, finally, a sense of place. As it turns out, true belonging is found only in the sovereign palm of God. There alone we find our place, even amid the seasons of moving, planting, uprooting, and replanting.

It's only when we find our place in Him that we find rest. David said it with beautiful simplicity:

I am at rest in God alone.
PSALM 62:1, CSB

Though the path to this discovery is often painful, the discovery itself can be a relief—and not only to us. It gives us space to spread out and grow, and it relieves our other loves of a burden too big to carry.

And there we can bear mysterious fruit.

CHAPTER 3

grapes

I didn't care a whit about grapes until Tuscany. I'd like to say that I did. I want to tell you that this has been a lifelong love affair and that my mother used to say, "That child ate her weight in grapes before she grew a single tooth in those gums." It would be lovely if I could make this all about God fulfilling my destiny, but that's not how it went.

Up until a year ago, I was of the smug opinion that the grape was embarrassingly outclassed by the cherry. The two fruits didn't even deserve to be in the same section of the grocery store. I also thought strawberries left grapes to rot. If I were forced to eat fruit, at least a strawberry could be dipped in chocolate. Give me the run of the produce section, and I'd have picked a watermelon over a grape every time.

Simply put, the grape disinterested me. In my opinion, it was the lemon of all fruits, including the lemon. That's a shameful admission on this side of all I've studied in the last months, because what I now intend to show you is that God seems to have a special place in His heart—and on the sacred page—for grapes.

+ + +

In a Christian retail world where study Bibles are available in innumerable specialized sorts, from *The Firefighter's Bible* to *The Grandmother's Bible*, a casual perusal of the mile-long list of plants in Scripture could make a soul wonder how on earth we've managed to bypass *The Botanist's Study Bible*. Search "plants" in a decent Bible dictionary, and you'll discover multiple pages landscaped in shrubs, grasses, herbs, stalks, flowers, and trees in a field so broad it reaches from *A* for *acacia* to, if not *Z*, then *W*, with the book of Revelation coming in strong with *wormwood*.

An industrious traveler across Scripture's fruited plains could eat her weight in almonds or, if she prefers mixed nuts, shake them up in a jar with walnuts and pistachios. If the nut route exceeds her maximum daily protein intake, she could eat her way across the Bible on nothing but grains. If carbs are a fate worse than death, she could feast on leeks, garlic, olives, and onions and then cure her breath with mint.

Should she step on a thorn, she could soothe her sore foot with aloes. If she breaks out in boils, she could make a fig poultice. If she comes upon a viper, she could whack it with a reed. Should she require a short siesta, she could doze amid the cattails. If her hair turns gray, she can touch it up with henna. At the end of her trek, she just might leave a lush field with the truest rose of Sharon and the lily of the valley.

In a Bible flourishing with plant life, no plant is given more space or frequency than the grapevine. Add each appearance of the word *grape* to its companion word *vineyard*, and their sum beats the olive tree, its closest contender, by a landslide. This despite the olive's well-earned status as an icon of the Mediterranean world. Give the grape her due, is all I'm saying. The ink was barely dry on "Let there be light" before the first mention of a vineyard in Genesis 9. Then, after rolling down the hallowed halls of both testaments, the grape takes its final bow in Scripture midway through the book of Revelation.

I know, I know. All of this begs the question, "So who cares?" Stay with me, and I hope to show you that we care because Jesus chose vines and vineyards for some of the most important imagery in our entire theology. These metaphors were no haphazard choices. They were distinct. Multilayered. Multipurpose. A lot is hidden under those grape skins.

In our quest for meaning, for a life that matters, the humble grape has volumes to say. Forgive my overenthusiasm, but there's power in that pulp. After studying the fruit of the vineyard, I found that my view of Christ's teachings had been completely recast. I'm just optimistic enough to believe it could do the same for you.

My purpose in this chapter is to give you a sweeping overview of the role of grapes and vineyards in Scripture, a panorama from cover to cover. In ensuing chapters of this book, we'll bring the lens in a little closer, but for now, let's go nice and wide.

The Bible's numerous references to grapes, vineyards, and vines span a wide range of uses. Sometimes the terms are as literal as the grapes I rinse under my kitchen faucet. Other times they are symbolic. Yet even within the symbolism category, they enjoy impressive diversity.

In Genesis 40:9-11, grapes serve as images in the chief cupbearer's dream, which he recounted to his cellmate Joseph, who interpreted them as good news of the cupbearer's imminent return to Pharaoh's service.

Grapes are also symbolic in their final appearance in Revelation. But rather than being warm and welcoming, their context here is chilling.

> *Another angel came out from the altar, the angel who has authority over the fire, and he called with a loud voice to the one who had the sharp sickle, "Put in your sickle and gather the clusters from the vine of the earth, for its grapes are ripe." So the angel swung his sickle across the earth and gathered the grape harvest of the earth and threw it into the great winepress of the wrath of God. And the winepress was trodden outside the city, and blood flowed from the winepress, as high as a horse's bridle, for 1,600 stadia.*
>
> REVELATION 14:18-20

The twentieth-century association of grapes with divine judgment rode in, not on the back of the Bible, but on the cover of John Steinbeck's Pulitzer Prize–winning novel *The Grapes of Wrath*. Ask someone my age and older with frugal knowledge of Scripture what grapes have to do with God, and the most popular answer will be "wrath." Without taking one whit from the symbolism in Revelation, however, the imagery of grape and vine carries more definitive themes elsewhere in the Bible.

To whet your appetite, here are a few appearances of either grapes or vines that carry considerable weight.

Perhaps the weightiest appearance, literally speaking, takes place when the Israelites are on the cusp of the Promised Land, after they had wandered in the desert for forty years. Nothing was random about the number forty. God assigned them one year of wandering for every day the Hebrew spies cased the good land yet had the gall to bring back a bad report:

We are not able to go up against the people, for they
are stronger than we are.

NUMBERS 13:31

Only Caleb and Joshua returned teeming with faith that God would do what He promised. Caleb's unflappable confidence is like heavily starched combat fatigues:

Let us go up at once and occupy it, for we are well able
to overcome it.

NUMBERS 13:30

Recently I read an article about a major study conducted by scholars at MIT Media Lab. Findings conveyed that on Twitter, false rumors traveled "farther, faster, deeper, and more broadly than the truth in all categories of information."[1] The study may have been limited to Twitter, but the phenomenon certainly isn't. It's as old as high school. Humans devour bad news. We may say we don't like it, but we click—and cluck—to the contrary.

Numbers 14 serves as a perfect exhibit of this phenomenon. The bad report took seed and grew like a sucker shoot into disaster fantasies.

All the congregation raised a loud cry, and the people wept
that night. And all the people of Israel grumbled against
Moses and Aaron. The whole congregation said to them,
"Would that we had died in the land of Egypt! Or would
that we had died in this wilderness! Why is the LORD
bringing us into this land, to fall by the sword? Our wives
and our little ones will become a prey. Would it not be better

Your fruit

WILL OUTLAST

YOUR LIFE.

for us to go back to Egypt?" And they said to one another,
"Let us choose a leader and go back to Egypt."

Then Moses and Aaron fell on their faces before all the
assembly of the congregation of the people of Israel. And
Joshua the son of Nun and Caleb the son of Jephunneh,
who were among those who had spied out the land, tore
their clothes and said to all the congregation of the people of
Israel, "The land, which we passed through to spy it out, is
an exceedingly good land. If the LORD delights in us, he will
bring us into this land and give it to us, a land that flows
with milk and honey. Only do not rebel against the LORD.
And do not fear the people of the land, for they are bread for
us. Their protection is removed from them, and the LORD is
with us; do not fear them." Then all the congregation said to
stone them with stones. But the glory of the LORD appeared
at the tent of meeting to all the people of Israel.

And the LORD said to Moses, "How long will this people
despise me? And how long will they not believe in me, in spite
of all the signs that I have done among them?"

NUMBERS 14:1-11

When God threatened to destroy the whole lot of them and
supply Moses with a greater and mightier nation, Moses interceded
and asked God to pardon their iniquity, just as He'd forgiven them
up until now (Numbers 14:19). God did forgive them, but He
sentenced the nation to forty years in the desert—sufficient time
for the skeletons of the faithless to accessorize the sand, picked
clean by jackals and bleached white by the glaring sun. Only Caleb
and Joshua outlived their peers and laid claim to the Promised
Land. Even the feet of Moses were never smudged with a single
particle of its soil.

There in the plains of Moab, on the brink of Canaan, Moses delivered final instructions to the Israelites, known to us as the book of Deuteronomy, before he climbed Mount Nebo and his extraordinary life ended. He reminded the Israelites of their humble history, their divine chosenness, and their renewed covenant with God. Like a preacher pounding a timber pulpit, he mustered them to faithfulness, declaring divine blessings for their obedience and curses galore for their disobedience.

Within the discourse, Moses depicted the land just beyond the Jordan in words replete with imagery enough to outshine a panoramic postcard.

> *The LORD your God is bringing you into a good land, a land of brooks of water, of fountains and springs, flowing out in the valleys and hills, a land of wheat and barley, of vines and fig trees and pomegranates, a land of olive trees and honey, a land in which you will eat bread without scarcity, in which you will lack nothing, a land whose stones are iron, and out of whose hills you can dig copper. And you shall eat and be full, and you shall bless the LORD your God for the good land he has given you.*
>
> DEUTERONOMY 8:7-10

Highlighter types like me can take sunny yellow ink to the eighth verse to mark each food that made the list and find exactly seven: wheat, barley, vines, figs, pomegranates, olives, and honey. Certainly the variety the land had to offer exceeded these seven items. The point was completeness. "You will lack nothing." Each agricultural product was also multipurpose, like the olive tree that produced not only fruit but also oil.

The land the Israelites would enter was a "good land."[2] This two-word description is meant to be memorable, making an appearance ten times in the book of Deuteronomy. I love any grain, wheat, or barley, especially when it turns into hot bread at the hands of a fine baker (and I humbly dare to say that I, on occasion, qualify). And nothing is better on a piece of toast the next morning than fig preserves. I could eat a pint of olives, be they green or purple, in one sitting, and I am gung ho about honey, though most scholars believe the honey in Deuteronomy 8:8 was pressed from dates rather than combed by bees. I am a fan of dates too, but primarily in theory rather than on the plate. Pomegranates, on the other hand, I relish. But were I God, I might have considered a seedless variety. How it would propagate, I do not know, but if I were God, I assume I would. All of this, of course, drives us to the cul-de-sac I have every intention of circling until we're dizzy: that of the vine.

Because the grape was proudly multipurpose, the shelf life it had to offer the ancient world was practically without rival. Grapes could be eaten fresh, straight from the vine. Dried, they were renamed raisins, and in the Bible, they were eaten plain or baked into cakes. Pressed, the grapes produced fresh juice, or far more significantly, they could be utterly transformed, possessing new properties and chemistry, into vinegars and wines.

In case your mind wandered as mine is wont to do, permit me to go at that again. Behold the extended-release capsule known as the common grape:

ripe grapes (for now) → dried grapes (for soon and later) and aged grapes (for later and still later)—fermented, pressed, and skinned until they flow with a liquid that can outlast a mortal lifetime

According to Scripture's favorite marriage counselor, raisins are essentials for the enthusiastic newlywed. After all, who had more practice when it came to marriage than Solomon?

Sustain me with raisins . . . for I am sick with love.
SONG OF SONGS 2:5

The grape is the consummate overachiever among fruits. Take its kernels and make grapeseed oil. Take its leaves, brined, boiled, and rinsed, and stuff them with a glorious concoction of rice, pine nuts, onions, parsley, dill, mint, salt, and pepper, then sauté them to perfection in olive oil, and *voilà! Dolmathakia!*

+ + +

The most famous grape sighting in the Old Testament is found in the same narrative we discussed earlier, when the spies returned with a bad report of the good land. The scene just prior to their negative tirade makes their whining all the whinier. I'll let Moses tell the story for himself. Don't miss a word of it.

Moses sent them to spy out the land of Canaan and said to them, "Go up into the Negeb and go up into the hill country, and see what the land is, and whether the people who dwell in it are strong or weak, whether they are few or many, and whether the land that they dwell in is good or bad, and whether the cities that they dwell in are camps or strongholds, and whether the land is rich or poor, and whether there are trees in it or not. Be of good courage and bring some of the fruit of the land." Now the time was the season of the first ripe grapes.

So they went up and spied out the land. . . . And they came
to the Valley of Eshcol and cut down from there a branch with
a single cluster of grapes, and they carried it on a pole between
two of them; they also brought some pomegranates and figs.
That place was called the Valley of Eshcol, because of the cluster
that the people of Israel cut down from there.

At the end of forty days they returned from spying out
the land. And they came to Moses and Aaron and to all the
congregation of the people of Israel in the wilderness of Paran,
at Kadesh. They brought back word to them and to all the
congregation, and showed them the fruit of the land. And
they told him, "We came to the land to which you sent us. It
flows with milk and honey, and this is its fruit. However, the
people who dwell in the land are strong, and the cities are
fortified and very large. And besides, we saw the descendants
of Anak there. The Amalekites dwell in the land of the
Negeb. The Hittites, the Jebusites, and the Amorites dwell in
the hill country. And the Canaanites dwell by the sea, and
along the Jordan."

But Caleb quieted the people before Moses and said,
"Let us go up at once and occupy it, for we are well able
to overcome it."

NUMBERS 13:17-21, 23-30

Grapes don't grow solo; they only grow in clusters. Scale the
world's finest hills and forge through her fertile valleys, and you'll
find their clusters in all sorts of colors—pink, purple, crimson,
green, black, dark blue, yellow, and orange—up to a mind-boggling
ten thousand varieties. Don't tell me that's not impressive.

The Hebrew word for "cluster" is *eshcol*. One branch with a
single cluster of grapes had to be carried by two grown men on

a pole between them—that's some kind of heavy fruit. One horticulturist suggests these grapes were of the Syrian variety known for producing clusters of between twenty and thirty pounds.[3] Whatever the variety, this much is certain: the fruit from the land of promise was weighty.

Thousands of years later, in that same land, a Vine grew, which from all outward appearances was common. The Vine made a promise to eleven branches—the Twelve minus Judas—if only they'd abide.

Much fruit. Heavy fruit. Weighty fruit. The most profitable fruit in all the world.

Now the time was the season of the first ripe grapes (Numbers 13:20).

Through Jesus Christ, you are in the bloodline of those very fruit bearers. Maybe you feel passed over. Invisible. Unviable. Maybe you believe that God calls other people to contribute and use their gifts for His noble purposes, but your own branch seems bare. Perhaps the last thing you feel like is the answer to a promise. Or perhaps the way it looks to you, at one time you showed great promise and your gifts were affirmed, but for some baffling reason, all that promise seemed to fizzle out and amount to nothing.

If that's you, then I want you to know that if you are in Christ, your life is attached to the very One who *is* life. Nothing about you means nothing, because He who defines you and makes use of you is everything. Your identity is in the One whose name reverberates above every other name and whose fame endures forever.

You aren't in this alone, either. You have brothers and sisters throughout the world. Your connectedness is unbreakable. You are part of a community of saints that all the demons in the entire abyss cannot overcome.

Your fruit will outlast your life. You can't always see the effects, because they are eternal, but one day you will. One day you will see that you couldn't have been more significant if you'd tried.

PART 2

The Vinedresser

Let me sing for my beloved
my love song concerning his vineyard:
My beloved had a vineyard
on a very fertile hill.

ISAIAH 5:1

CHAPTER 4

song

Not long ago I got to hear poet Christian Wiman read his poetry. I attended the event with my daughter Melissa, as Wiman is one of her favorite writers, and she is one of my favorite thinkers. The setting would have made a concert of sixth-grade saxophone players tolerable. We were a quaint crowd, tucked in a limestone lodge in the Texas Hill Country at autumn's high tide, when trees were arrogant with fierce color and city sounds so far removed I could hear stems of plate-sized leaves snapping loose from their limbs.

The lodge leans over a clear, slender river the color of an old Sprite bottle hit just right by the sun, a sight to be savored from slow rocking chairs on the porch. One has ample time for such lingering there since Wi-Fi is available only at the registration desk in a space roughly the size of a bathroom stall, but with more pleasant ambience. The rooms in our building weren't numbered. They were named for poets. I stayed in Browning while Melissa was next door with Tennyson. And the coffee was good. No venue on earth is good enough for poor coffee.

Wiman, a professor at Yale, shared a bit of his story, and I thought how utterly free he seemed to be of any lust for the limelight. I didn't get the idea that he was unimpressed with us but rather that he was unimpressed with himself, a quality I find wholly irresistible in an orator. He has the gift of depth at gargantuan cost, having stared down the chalky-gray throat of death at the peak of his years and managed to hang on to the lip.

A sucker for an autobiography, I would have been content if all the poet had done was talk about his tumultuous love affair with poetry. That's not what he did. After fifteen minutes of telling his story, he read to us. No, he recited to us. He recited what his own pen had broken open and bled onto the page. We were ticket holders to a transfiguration, not of Wiman's form, but of his speech. The phrases rumbled and thundered, not with volume but with force. They were not so heavy with articulation that the hearer missed the art.

I don't just like words. I like syllables, too, and this was a man who knew how to use them. Some consonants had hard stops, like the sharp heel of a shoe smacking granite tile. Others slid and tumbled and rolled as if the edges had been erased with the pink end of a soft lead pencil. The lines were rhythmic but not predictable—think rhythmic in the way of a sycamore leaf tumbling across the grass in breezes and gusts. Poetry is music to those who don't require singing to have a song. Wiman's variety was no routine scale up a treble staff where "Every good boy does fine." These notes came from the bass staff, from what the New

Testament writers called *tá splágchna*—the viscera or, for those who can stomach it, the intestines. The bowels.

We think in terms of the depths of the heart, but any surgeon can testify there is no heart so deep as the bowels.

Isaiah was a poet, as most of the Old Testament prophets were. We'll see that God used him to put to paper the most iconic verses on God's vineyard in the stretch from Genesis to Malachi—verses that almost certainly loom large in the backdrop of Christ's teaching on the vine and branches. This passage in Isaiah is a key to unlocking the bigger picture of the vineyard throughout Scripture, so we'll spend a little time here with the prophet and his song of the vineyard.

Whether or not Isaiah was a poet before God took hold of him, he'd earned his literary diploma by the time the ink dried on the sixty-sixth chapter of the book called by his name. With the exception of chapters 6–8 and the historical interlude found in chapters 36–39, the hand of God pushed the pen across the scroll of Isaiah almost entirely in Hebrew poetry.

The miracles etched on the pages of Isaiah's prophecies have unexpected twists and turns, lest a reader think God works His wonders by rote. In Genesis, the barren land gives birth. In Isaiah, the virgin gives birth. In Exodus, God lays bare a veritable strip of desert in the sea so the Israelites can cross on dry land. He performs the freshwater version of the same wonder in Joshua as He leads them from the wilderness through a parted river into the Promised Land. But watch the reverse in Isaiah, where God Himself draws the contrast.

> *"I am the LORD, your Holy One,*
> *the Creator of Israel, your King."*

Thus says the LORD,
    who makes a way in the sea,
    a path in the mighty waters . . .
"Remember not the former things,
    nor consider the things of old.
Behold, I am doing a new thing;
    now it springs forth, do you not perceive it?
I will make a way in the wilderness
    and rivers in the desert."

ISAIAH 43:15-16, 18-19

Did you catch the last line—"rivers in the desert"? It is an intentional reversal of what God accomplished in the days of Moses and Joshua, when He put a strip of desert, we might say, in the middle of the waters to give His people passage on dry ground. The turnabout stirs up an inquiry of sorts. Do you think all tomorrow's wonders will look like yesterday's? Do you think divine deliverance always happens the same way? Do you imagine the Creator of heaven and earth is satisfied to stifle His creativity?

Do you, Beth?

I want to say no. I want to believe no. But aren't we all prone to assume yes?

Skeptics of Isaiah's divine inspiration would have had to muffle their ears to fail to hear Jesus repeatedly stamping it with approval in the Gospels. Matthew, Mark, Luke, and John record eight occasions when Jesus quoted Isaiah and a brow-raising number of occasions when He Himself fulfilled Isaiah's prophecies.

In His own hometown, Jesus launched His public ministry by blatantly owning the job description recorded in the opening verses of Isaiah 61. He was so clear about His intent that the enraptured crowd soon became enraged and attempted to shove Him off a cliff. There was no mincing of words here:

He came to Nazareth, where he had been brought up. And as was his custom, he went to the synagogue on the Sabbath day, and he stood up to read. And the scroll of the prophet Isaiah was given to him. He unrolled the scroll and found the place where it was written,

"The Spirit of the Lord is upon me,
    because he has anointed me
    to proclaim good news to the poor.
He has sent me to proclaim liberty to the captives
    and recovering of sight to the blind,
    to set at liberty those who are oppressed,
to proclaim the year of the Lord's favor."

And he rolled up the scroll and gave it back to the attendant and sat down. And the eyes of all in the synagogue were fixed on him. And he began to say to them, "Today this Scripture has been fulfilled in your hearing."

LUKE 4:16-21

For me, the prominent historical figures in the Bible seem more like people and less like legends if I try to picture what they might have looked like. To help me grasp Isaiah as the poet-prophet he was, I'm choosing to picture him a bit like Christian Wiman, the poet who led the event Melissa and I attended.

I have to tweak a few things. For instance, Isaiah would need considerably more hair—at least to his shoulders, in my mind's eye—and undoubtedly it would be gray, wavy, and unruly. He'd look a little wild eyed, I think, since his eyes had "seen the King, the LORD of hosts" and the sight had, in his own words, undone him and caused him to yowl, "Woe is me!" (Isaiah 6:5). There would be no getting over that—I have to believe it would show on his face.

I feel certain that Isaiah's robe would be in a wad a good bit of the time too. I'm pretty sure most people who serve an unseen God for enough years, trying their danged hardest to obey His inaudible directions and love His confounding people with their own contorted hearts, live a quarter-inch from sheer madness much of the time. But maybe that's just me.

Wiman never once broke into song while reciting his poetry to us, though I wouldn't have minded if he had. Isaiah, on the other hand, did indeed. Exactly once. And that one time is the precise place the vine theme of his book starts taking root. This is how the song opens:

> Let me sing for my beloved
>   my love song concerning his vineyard:
> My beloved had a vineyard
>   on a very fertile hill.
>
> ISAIAH 5:1

God is referenced by more than thirty different names in Isaiah's sixty-six chapters. Among them are Lord Almighty, Shepherd, Potter, Redeemer, Creator, King, Savior, Rock, Rock Eternal, Judge, Lawgiver, and Warrior. Here in Isaiah 5? *My beloved.* The prophet opens his mouth and sings a song for his beloved in what is unmistakably the most tender and telling insight into the prophet that can be found with a fine-tooth comb in his voluminous document.

Feel the tone change. Hemmed in by the highest, loftiest

references to God in all of holy writ, Isaiah shifts keys and writes a song for his *beloved*. So, yes, *feel* it. A love song unfelt is unfit. Some poems are penned to make you think. Love songs are meant to make you feel. And then, if they're worth the price of a guitar string, to think.

And so it is for us. If you find that you have lost the song somewhere along the way—if you are going through the motions with Jesus but it's dwindled to duty and lost all delight—take a moment and soak this in: as surely as Isaiah sang to his beloved, the God of heaven sings love songs over you.

David sang to God in one of his psalms,

You are my hiding place;
*   you will protect me from trouble*
*   and surround me with songs of deliverance.*

PSALM 32:7, NIV

Try to absorb the wonder of it: we have a soundtrack playing over us, proclaiming our deliverance. Here we are, down under, feeling unseen while we're being watched over by the King of heaven and surrounded by singers our ears are not yet tuned to hear.

In the next line of the psalm, God sings back: "I will instruct you and teach you in the way you should go; I will counsel you with my loving eye on you" (Psalm 32:8, NIV). Countless times, I've considered that our songs of praise join with those of the angels encircling God's throne. But the psalmist, under the very inspiration of God, records numerous lines of the Lord Himself singing over His people.

Can you imagine? Think of all the times you've sung to God in worship. Has it ever occurred to you that, when you take a breath, He just might be singing back?

This notion would have been familiar to the prophet Zechariah, who wrote these lines from the mouth of God:

> *On that day it shall be said to Jerusalem:*
> *"Fear not, O Zion;*
>   *let not your hands grow weak.*
> *The LORD your God is in your midst,*
>   *a mighty one who will save;*
> *he will rejoice over you with gladness;*
>   *he will quiet you by his love;*
> *he will exult over you with loud singing."*
>
> ZEPHANIAH 3:16-17

Loud singing. I like that part. You don't sing loudly over someone you're ashamed of. I've spent so much of my life wondering if God was ashamed of me. I won't scandalize you with all the reasons why, but you can trust me on this: they're legitimate. If I got what I earned, He would be ashamed of me. Maybe you feel like that's what you earned too, but neither of us got what we deserved.

The book of Hebrews drops the shame off of us like a ragged cloak that no longer fits:

> *The one who sanctifies and those who are sanctified all*
> *have one Father. That is why Jesus is not ashamed to*
> *call them brothers and sisters.*
>
> HEBREWS 2:11, CSB

Just two verses later, the writer of Hebrews records Jesus announcing, "Here I am with the children God gave me." For the life of me, I can't find a single note of shame in that statement.

CHRIST'S LOVE
FOR YOU IS
UTTERLY

shameless.

True, Hebrews doesn't say that Jesus sang this line. He spoke it. But make no mistake, Jesus sang with His disciples (Matthew 26:30). Songs were an integral part of the Jewish feasts and annual pilgrimages. And you know Jesus has to sing well. It's unthinkable that the One who created song wouldn't set a high bar for singing.

Truthfully, however, it wouldn't matter to me if He didn't sing well. As long as He sang loud and proud, He'd have me in the palm of His hand. There's a great scene in the late nineties movie *My Best Friend's Wedding* when the jealous antagonist (played by Julia Roberts) tries to set up her rival (played by Cameron Diaz) for failure. Roberts's character traps her into singing karaoke at the rehearsal dinner before a packed house. She's terrible. Tone deaf. And loud. But the plan to humiliate her backfires because her pure willingness to get up there and own her affection for her beloved wins not only him but everyone else in the crowd. It doesn't matter how off key she is; she's in love.

Sometimes nothing's more beautiful than being a fool for love. Nothing makes life feel more alive than knowing you're loved—especially knowing you're loved with unblushing abandon.

And that's what you need to know most of all—that Christ's love for you is utterly shameless. And He is no fool.

✦ ✦ ✦

Sometimes you know from the first few notes that a song is going to rip your heart out. Words aren't necessary. Let a single cello lead the way into a melody, and several bars in, it becomes a fellow mourner, sitting beside you in your grief. Never mind that you have no clue what you're grieving. Before the last note, you will think of something.

Music wields a power words alone can rarely match. It sidesteps your defenses and comes for you without politely asking permission. If you don't know to dig in your heels, it can drag you where you had no intention of going.

Other times you settle in for a feel-good song and it does you wrong. This sort ropes you in with lyrics. It tells you you're pretty and makes you feel good. You lean in and turn it up. Then midway it changes its tune and tells you, "Pretty is as pretty does," and if the song knows wrong from right, you may be pretty ugly after all. If the song happens to be sung by a guitar-strumming prophet, the next stanza will very likely tell you what happens next if you don't change your hideous ways.

Cue the words of Isaiah's song again:

Let me sing for my beloved
my love song concerning his vineyard:
My beloved had a vineyard
on a very fertile hill.

Oh, please do, Isaiah. By all means. Who can resist a love song, especially one in this echelon? The pastoral landscape is welcoming and wooing. We're perfectly content to let the song take us there. Let's curl up close to the speaker and allow the coming stanza to transport us.

He dug it and cleared it of stones,
and planted it with choice vines;
he built a watchtower in the midst of it,
and hewed out a wine vat in it;
and he looked for it to yield grapes.
ISAIAH 5:2

So far, so good. We love songs that tell us what love has done for us, what trouble love has gone to on our behalf. How worth it we must be!

Then Isaiah's song turns on a dime.

At my house, this is the scene: Keith and I are conspiring in the kitchen toward a feast of Moore proportions, using every pan within his long arm's reach. Music is playing on a Bluetooth speaker on the counter next to the stove. A song starts up, sweet and delicious. It's new to us, but we like it already, and three bars in, we're under its spell. We let the gravy bubble and leave the bread half-buttered to break into a spontaneous two-step. It's all ribbons and romance, meter and rhyme. Then, midway through the song, one of us trips over the other's feet, elbow hitting the skillet handle, knocking the pan to the tile floor, shooting up gravy like a geyser. This sends us running for cover because one thing is clear: somebody is about to get burned.

I guess this is as good a time as any to admit to hearing Isaiah's folk song for his Beloved in pure country—and not because I prefer the genre. I don't. It's because a country-western song can start you out at a family picnic eating buttermilk-fried chicken and watermelon on your great-grandmother's quilt, with butterflies flitting about, and before it ends, your daddy's gone to prison and your momma's run off with the preacher and your little brother's blowing butterflies to dust with a BB gun.

In Isaiah's song of the vineyard, the first indication of a change to a minor key accompanies these five words: "But it yielded wild grapes" (Isaiah 5:2).

Wild isn't so bad, we figure. In fact, we like the thought of being wild. Untamable and free spirited are enshrined qualities in a culture of individualists. If we're not going to live up to expectations, let it be because we're wild at heart. But in this passage, the meaning of the word translated "wild" carries wider connotations than being untamable. It can also mean sour, bitter, unripe, worthless, or even rotten. But the most insulting interpretation of all is "stinking."

There's a certain romance to being naughty, but none of us wants to stink. Sensory meanings tend to be taken personally. It's like your mother asking you if you remembered your deodorant. The most natural reaction is defensiveness. And defensiveness is best played with blame casting. "If I didn't turn out well, it's because you didn't treat me well."

The text anticipates our excuse and will answer to it before we can get a word in edgewise.

+ + +

Many Bible commentators nod over the strong possibility that this parable is casting Isaiah in the role of troubadour, or friend of the bridegroom. As a means of relating to Isaiah as the troubadour, a natural place to start is with "best man," as long as we allow his role to burgeon well beyond keeping the wedding ring handy in his coat pocket during the ceremony.

In fact, go ahead and place the negotiations of the entire marriage contract in his hands.[1] Pile on the role of the intermediary between the bride and the groom, who customarily had no direct contact before marriage. If the groom had misgivings about the bride, they were officially registered with her by—you guessed it— the friend of the bridegroom.

Imagine a typical rehearsal dinner in our culture. The best man stands to give a toast and say a few words about the couple, but with the emphasis on the groom, his dearest friend. Pretend he's a musician who crafts his words into melodies rather than speech. He sets the glass down and picks up the microphone, the one with the portable speaker. He taps the mic to make sure it's working and then begins to sing.

The lyrics start out warm—beautiful and romantic, because this is precisely how the couple's story began. But what the best man knows that the audience hasn't grasped is that the bride hasn't only acted unfaithfully to the groom. She has acted selfishly, wrongly, unjustly, and even criminally to him and to many others.

The friend of the bridegroom (or best man, in our tale) makes it no further than "wild grapes" when suddenly the groom himself stands to his feet, slips the microphone from the troubadour's hand, and takes over the song.

> *And now, O inhabitants of Jerusalem*
>   *and men of Judah,*
> *judge between me and my vineyard.*
> *What more was there to do for my vineyard,*
>   *that I have not done in it?*
> *When I looked for it to yield grapes,*
>   *why did it yield wild grapes?*
>
> ISAIAH 5:3-4

Exactly how rotten and putrid was the fruit? The seventh verse bleeds the grape:

> *For the vineyard of the LORD of hosts*
>   *is the house of Israel,*
> *and the men of Judah*
>   *are his pleasant planting;*

and he looked for justice,
but behold, bloodshed;
for righteousness,
but behold, an outcry!

ISAIAH 5:7

The song goes on for twenty-three more verses, but one question shimmers hauntingly throughout the lyrics, refusing to be forgotten:

What more was there to do for my vineyard, that I have not done in it?

The willing hearer knows the answer. *Nothing.*

+   +   +

There is no song like a song of unrequited love. Everyone knows one. Most everyone has one. It can play anywhere—at a party, in a restaurant, in a salon, over the sound system in a store—and suddenly you're right back in that moment. Feeling sick inside. Jolted. Perhaps you fish the song back out on purpose because something has you remembering. You replay it because you wonder now, after all this time, if it was real.

It was. You know by how long it takes you to shake out of the replay after the music stops. We have nothing more intimate to offer another living soul than our love. Authentic affection cannot exist apart from vulnerability. A heart that is wide open to love is wide open to hurt. We could seal off our hearts in an attempt to avoid being hurt, but in doing so, we'd also shut ourselves off from relationships that make life matter.

No one is exempt from the pain of rejection, not even God. No, I'll push that further: *especially* not God.

He is, after all, the author, eternal possessor, initiator, and giver of love. He cannot be destroyed or made less by unrequited love, but to disassociate Him from the pain and grief associated with love is to carve a convenient idol out of wood or stone bearing no resemblance to the God of the Bible. Within those pages, we find a God who cannot be changed by man but can be affected by man. His immutability does not deplete or delete His affections.

God is described with a wide range of responsive emotions toward us humans: delight, pleasure, displeasure, anger, compassion, laughter, pity, grief, and sorrow, to name a few. Jealousy and wrath are among the most unsettling emotions attributed to God, because sinless versions of either one are unfathomable to us. The titanic difference between God's affections and ours is that His are incorruptible. We process information about Him as if His emotions were created in our image rather than ours in His image. The original source of all emotion is utterly undefiled.

Jesus, in whom "all the fullness of God was pleased to dwell," fleshed out further complexity and color on the palette of divine emotion. Jesus, who could read human thoughts (Luke 6:8; 11:17), could also marvel at a human's faith (Luke 7:9) and lack of faith (Mark 6:6). He is depicted as rejoicing in the Holy Spirit in direct response to humans (Luke 10:21). He celebrated, sorrowed, wept, and ached. He experienced churning turmoil in the depths of His soul over humanity and felt the scorching sting of betrayal and rejection. He also knew the misery of dread (Matthew 26:39).

One of the most mysterious aspects about God communicated in Scripture is that His knowledge about what would transpire didn't necessarily preclude His heightened hopes of something different. He didn't always spare Himself the shock of something appalling, even though He saw it coming. Even a predestined conclusion didn't spare God the emotion of the result. Perhaps most significantly, *knowing* why didn't keep God from *asking* why (Isaiah 5:4 and Mark 15:34).

In Isaiah's song, God watches and waits with anxious expectation for His choice vine—desired, planned, prepared for, and planted by hand—to bring forth fruit. And it did.

But it was rotten fruit.

CHAPTER 5

inspection

Years ago, when the number of attendees at Living Proof Live events started swelling—and, consequently, scaring me half to death—I decided that God would be most honored, and I'd be most reliant on Him if I fasted from the time each conference began until after it ended. If effectiveness increased in response to the combination of fasting and praying, as Scripture indicated it did, why wouldn't the same formula work for fasting and speaking?

It made perfect sense to me, so I kept this up for years—not one bite on an event weekend, from Friday after lunch until Saturday afternoon. Twenty-four hours or so was plenty doable. After all, some saints fast for days on end. Admittedly, they're not much fun on a lunch date, but I respect them to no end. Anyway, I desperately needed God to show up. The way I saw it, God would be more likely to demonstrate favor at events if I fasted.

Never mind that favor can't be earned. Never mind that there is no formula on earth for guaranteeing the outpouring of God's Spirit. Sometimes we're wheeling and dealing and calling it holy. The longer I live, the less I find God to be a hand shaker. Hand holder? Yes. Hand shaker? No.

God was faithful. He can be no other way. He carried me through each of those events, especially in the last few hours, when I felt shaky, and afterward, when the meet-and-greet would go on until I was nearly in tears. I'd already given everything I had. I don't play when I teach. I throw my whole body into it.

Then I started seeing stars. Sometimes during the last session, I'd have to steady myself at the podium for a moment until the lightheadedness passed. I was so depleted at the end of an event that the aftereffects weren't just physical. I'd immediately face spiritual attack, as if a hoard of demonic spider monkeys were jumping on my back.

Wait a minute, I thought. *Isn't fasting supposed to make us more effective at warfare?* Isn't that what Jesus was implying when His disciples couldn't deliver the demon-possessed kid and Jesus told them, "This kind does not go out except by prayer and fasting" (Matthew 17:21, NKJV)?

I was in it to win it, so I decided I just needed to pray more. I'd made a commitment, and I wouldn't break it. What if God withdrew His Spirit?

If this sounds like madness to you, welcome to the life of someone so far out on a limb, she felt like she had only the space of a twig to mess up. I was going to keep it up if it killed me.

Then at one event, right in the energetic throes of the final session, I thought it was indeed going to. The whole place went dark. By God's grace, my vision blacked out only for a second, and beyond the notice of the audience, but I can tell you this: I started eating. I've done so ever since, and as far as I can tell, God is still coming to the events. He hadn't told me to fast while I served with every ounce of my being. I'd volunteered to do it out of devotion. It was a godly idea that didn't produce good fruit.

This turned out to be one of the most important lessons I've ever learned. If I can be used by God to convey this message to you before you black out in your own destructive way, we'll have accomplished something worthwhile. Something holy.

+ + +

Only one thing is worse than producing no fruit: producing bad fruit. Let there be no mistaking that people of God, the chosen branches of the perfect Vine, can bear unripe, sour, bitter, rotten, and foul-smelling fruit. I've done it. I've also seen it, smelled it, and eaten it. We can even be moral and religiously upright and produce rotten fruit.

Jesus accused the Pharisees of doing exactly that. Some among them zealously defended the letter of the law but with such self-righteous pride and lovelessness that their fruit was sufficiently sour to lock the loosest jaw.

What's confusing to a world full of amateur fruit inspectors is how similar a bitter grape can look to a sweet one. The world gets a bad taste in its mouth and loses its appetite for grapes entirely, casting all fruit of the vine into the same basket. After a while, the whole grape cart starts stinking to high heaven under a cloud of happy fruit flies.

The thing about good fruit is that it can't be faked. Sometimes our goal for bearing immense fruit is to have a camera-ready table display—to be seen, noticed, marveled over. This kind of branding is so prevalent that we're no longer sure we know the difference. But this is grotesquely incongruent with the gospel.

If we want to resist the temptation to promote more good than we actually perform, we'll have to be deliberate. Fruit is to be eaten, or it will rot. The only fruit that lasts indefinitely without being eaten is the plastic kind.

Since the Father calls Jesus-followers to live immensely fruitful lives, it stands to reason that no question is more relevant than this: What kind of fruit are we producing? We can't see fruit the way God can, but with His help, we are fully capable of distinguishing between good fruit and bad fruit.

Inspection becomes an act of obedience, and no one has more at stake in the analysis than a leader. Whether or not you see yourself as such, this I can assure you with a fair amount of confidence: if you are in active pursuit of knowing, loving, and adoring Jesus, and "press[ing] on toward the goal for the prize of the upward call of God in Christ Jesus" (Philippians 3:14), you are either an active leader or an emerging one. Your breed is so countercultural, it will not go unnoticed in your sphere of influence, whether by a few or by many.

Ever since I began chasing vines in Tuscany, I've been increasingly analyzing the quality of some of the fruit coming from my own life and leadership. Would you be willing to risk making this question part of your frequent vocabulary too?

Is what I'm doing (this action, approach, example,
or instruction) bearing good fruit?

Let's set the question in a couple of different contexts to make the inquiry more applicable. Keep in mind, we're not just on the hunt for bad fruit. We're also on the lookout for good fruit. If we think we have a God who only convicts and never encourages, who only tells us what's wrong with us and never what's right, we've probably created a god made in the image of a human authority who scarred us. We're safe and loved by God, no matter what kind of fruit we're currently producing.

- What kind of *good* fruit have I produced in my marriage and my family? My local church? My community?
- What kind of *bad* fruit have I produced in my marriage and my family? My local church? My community?
- What *bad* fruit have I produced through my job or calling? What *good* fruit have I produced?
- What fruit—good and bad—have I produced through my leisure time activities or hobbies?
- Has my social life borne good fruit or bad fruit?

What's the best way to tell what kind of fruit is being produced in your life? Look for evidence of the fruit of the Spirit—things like "love, joy, peace, patience, kindness, goodness, faithfulness, gentleness, [and] self-control" (Galatians 5:22-23). If the action or approach is quenching qualities of the Spirit, it's producing bad fruit. If it's evidencing qualities of the Spirit, it's producing good fruit.

A few questions like these might help us with our self-evaluation:

- Is my heart growing warmer or colder toward people?
- Am I constantly in a bad mood?
- Am I increasingly exhausted?
- Do I get fixated on offenses, or am I willing to overlook most of them?
- Have I become harsher or gentler over the last year?
- Do I lose control easily?

Determining what kind of fruit we're producing often requires nuance. For example, has making a particular decision caused challenges or chaos? Obstacles and hardships are normative in our lives. Opposition can be too. Ongoing chaos, however, is a different matter. When peace seems to have vacated the premises, the scent of rotten fruit is usually in the air.

None of us can do everything. None of us can please everyone. None of us has access to more than twenty-four hours a day or to more than seven days a week. By God's design, these mortal bodies are fraught with limits and bound by certain natural laws. If we don't eat, we starve. If we don't sleep, we die. If we don't ever stop, we drop. If we abandon what we're doing to answer every text, we'll never finish any significant task. None of us is the exception. None of us can do a thousand things to the glory of God, but we can do several. When you're on your deathbed, which ones will you want to have chosen?

My answers may sound typical or even trite, but I'll risk throwing them out there anyway. I want to love Jesus with my whole heart, mind, soul, and strength. I want him to be able to say, "Man, that girl just would not quit." I want my grandchildren to have a real, live grandmother who knows when they have tests at school or when they have a cold. I want to be their emergency contact after their parents because I'm always close at hand. I want my husband to say, "I would have chosen her again, knowing it all." I want ten thousand conversations with my daughters on the back porch. I want them to say, standing over my casket, "Mom was so funny." I want Jesus, and I want my family. That's what I will want most in the end.

Have guts enough to choose the things that matter now.

The fact that Christ calls every follower into some realm of active discipleship (Matthew 28:18-20) floats this question toward the top of the fruit-analysis list for all of us (at least, for those who aren't newborns in the faith):

Are people I'm helping disciple actually being discipled?

In order to maximize the benefit of this analysis, resist letting yourself off the hook with quick responses and generalities. Get specific. Get personal. Picture faces. Grab a sheet of paper or use the margin and name names.

Is good fruit being produced in the believing lives of a significant number of those who sit under the influence of your teaching, mentoring, leading, counseling, advising, preaching, spiritual parenting, or big brothering or sistering? You may not see yourself as a leader, but let me assure you—you have a sphere of influence, whether it's your family, your neighborhood, your church, or your group of friends.

In order to answer this question with accuracy, specifics are helpful:

- Are those under your purposeful influence growing in any discernible ways in their love for God and neighbor?
- Are they maturing in their witness, as far as you can tell?
- Have they begun to serve God and others instead of being content to watch you serve God and them?
- Is their discipleship personal rather than primarily social?
- To the degree that you are able to observe, does their life bear the fruit of forgiveness and demonstrate love?
- Are their relationships improving?

First, look to those who were infants in faith when they came under your influence. Has there been growth? Are they toddling? Are some walking? Even running? Next, look to the ones who came under your influence when they were already fairly discipled. Has their fervor been sustained? Has it grown?

HAVE GUTS
ENOUGH TO CHOOSE
THE THINGS THAT
matter now.

As I have pondered these questions from the perspective of a teacher, I drew one question straight from Jeremiah:

Let the prophet who has a dream tell the dream, but let him who has my word speak my word faithfully. What has straw in common with wheat? declares the LORD.

JEREMIAH 23:28

I frequently ask myself (sometimes ruthlessly) if I've served mostly straw or wheat—in other words, if my teaching has real substance or if it is stuffed with filler that won't stand the test of time. To keep the question on my radar, I've written the phrase "Straw or wheat?" randomly throughout the blank pages of my journal.

The necessary disclaimer in all this talk about fruit analysis is that those under our discipleship bear responsibility for their own fruitfulness. If they are not receptive or responsive, their lack of fruit is self-imposed. The focus of this present discourse, however, is not on a lack of fruit. It's on bad fruit.

+ + +

Many years ago, I came to the unpleasant realization that my legalism wasn't producing good fruit in my marriage. I came to a place where I was living out some measure of what Solomon meant by the peculiar words in Ecclesiastes:

Do not be excessively righteous and do not be overly wise. Why should you ruin yourself? Do not be excessively wicked and do not be a fool. Why should you die before your time?

ECCLESIASTES 7:16-17, NASB

How on earth is it possible to be "excessively righteous"? "Overly wise"? To be sure, righteousness and wisdom aren't the problem, since they rate high on Scripture's top-shelf priorities for God's people. The troublemakers are the adverbs, as they often are. *Excessively. Overly.*

I'll throw an example on the table. Keith and I both come from backgrounds of such darkness and depravity that I vigorously attempted to overcorrect us out of everything except G and PG movies. My husband has never been one to overcorrect well. For instance, my attempt to nip his profanity in the bud only made it grow into a veritable sequoia.

Keith doesn't know many Scriptures from memory, but he has thrown a paraphrase of Romans 7:23 at me more times than I can count: "You know the law does nothing but cause a war in my members." The actual verse goes like this: "I see another law in my members, warring against the law of my mind, and bringing me into captivity to the law of sin which is in my members" (KJV).

When Keith does a Bible throw-down, he always goes King James on me. I have accused him of preferring it because he dearly loves to quote verses with off-color words, and it offers a smattering. The King James Version makes fine and unsparing use of the word *dung*, for instance, where some of the more modern versions snub it altogether. Why none of the zealous proponents of KJV-only have never mentioned that disparity, I'll never know. Keith is particularly fond of the KJV for its alternative for *donkey*. This is my life. And, if you have any insight at all, you might pause and thank God that it is.

Might it be fair to say that my intentions were purer than Keith's? Maybe, but ironically, if I'd had my way on a legalistically righteous home, my efforts would not have produced good fruit. For one thing, I couldn't have kept it up. I was too broken, and I grasped too little about grace and the work of the Holy Spirit to keep from derailing.

The sincerest vows of the disfigured heart inevitably beg for self-sabotage. For another thing, forcing God down the gullets of family members does not leave a sweet taste in their mouths. That Keith and I instead kicked against the other's extremes, forcing a bit of balance in our home, did, in fact, produce good fruit. We still argue when we feel like the other goes too far, but we mostly dwell somewhere in the in-between, where saints still know they're sinners but don't forget they're saints.

The vantage point for evaluating fruit is one of the inestimable gifts of time. It's a simple equation. Fill in the first blank with virtually any practice, action, or approach. Fill in the second blank with the most fitting adjective.

$$\underline{\hspace{3cm}} + \text{TIME} = \underline{\hspace{3cm}} \text{FRUIT}$$

Legalism + TIME = *Grouchy* FRUIT

I look with piqued attention to those in the faith who are in their seventies, eighties, and nineties because I want to age well and joyfully, keeping fiery faith and fiery love for Jesus, for the Scriptures, and for fellow human beings. The fact that legalism ages irritably, if not miserably, has been, for me, an inescapable conclusion. If I may be so bold, it is not unusual for it to leave a permanent snarl upon the old saint's face.

The most prominent common denominator I've observed in Jesus-followers who appear to age joyfully is fullness of the Holy Spirit. Simply put, the health of their souls and their attentiveness to the things of the Spirit manage to outshine the decline of their bodies. It also seems to leave a permanent mark. Their faces are lined with kindness, and their eyes sparkle and easily fill with tears upon the mention of the name of Jesus.

Racial inequality + TIME = *Deadly* FRUIT

"Separate but equal" is largely a fallacy, if not an outright oxymoron. "Distinctive and equal" is a different story, but the mouth that incessantly professes the advantages of separatism can't help but exhale the noxious air of supremacy. Supremacy among mortals is always oppositional to God, but among people who carry the name of Christ, it is blasphemous.

Jesus alone is supreme. In His economy, the mark of greatness is worn only by the servant to all. Under Jesus' reign, the self-exalted are ultimately humbled and the self-humbled are ultimately exalted.

America has had a front-row seat to view the deadly fruit of ethnic injustice—and no less in the church than in the world. Many would argue that the church has historically offered racism its most audacious platforms. No one sees the sacred virtue in separate but equal like someone wearing the horse blinders of religious zeal.

Pervasive gender exclusivity + TIME = *unripe and rotten* FRUIT

"Separate but equal" produces similarly poisonous fruit in most issues of gender and eases its conscience with "distinctive but equal." We can clip two clusters of grapes from a single vine and hang them side by side, but if, during the growing process, one hangs so heavily and superiorly over the other that it eclipses the sun, the fruit of the underling naturally pales in comparison.

We could blame the cluster's poor production on its inherent inferiority, but it came from the same vine in the same field. The more likely cause is that another cluster loomed so large that it blocked the other from flourishing.

"Separate but equal" makes statements that are understandably hard to marry:

"We respect you; we just don't want you."
"We know you have a voice. We just don't want to hear it."
"We see you over there. Just stay over there."

God created male and female with an intricate balance of sameness and distinction, an impressive concoction of common part and counterpart.

Each image bearers.
Each of equal worth.
Each necessary for a future.
Each necessary for *survival*.

Where they differ, each is meant to help the other thrive. Roles can differ without sacrificing mutual respect, but it won't be accidental. Healthy relationships between brothers and sisters in Christ must be sought, fought for, and sacrificed for. Men and women who are never actively discipled together and who rarely serve near or next to one another will not just fail to develop respect for one another; they will be emotionally, relationally, and conversationally impaired toward one another.

Separatism produces bad fruit. I've observed it, experienced it, added to it, been complicit in it, watched it, read about it, heard about it, and seen evidence of it for far too long to dismiss any further.

Worshiping in the same room and hearing the same sermon

several times a month is woefully inadequate for promoting healthy relationships between the sexes. Pervasive gender exclusivity in the organic development of the church does not—indeed, it cannot—bear ripe fruit, because half of what is required for maturity is all but missing. It's tantamount to slicing the body of Christ at the waist and dividing it pound for pound. We could claim each half got their share, but the body would still be in pieces.

+   +   +

The good news is that it doesn't take years on end to do the math of our fruit-bearing equation. And it shouldn't, lest it prove too late in any given field to produce a different crop. All it takes is time enough. One annual cycle of four seasons was often sufficient for a vinedresser.

A parent willing to confront the truth of having driven a child too hard sees evidence of marred fruit long before the son or daughter launches. There's time to own the problem and address it humbly and openly with the child and develop a different dynamic, even if this sometimes requires outside help. Respect will be won, not lost. If the child is grown, it's not too late to go back and say, "I was too hard on you, and I am deeply sorry."

Friendships can change, and so can work environments and service organizations, if we're willing to face any bad fruit resulting from our approach. Don't shift the blame. And don't wait to deal with bad fruit. It won't improve on its own.

The caveat is whether we're able or willing to see clearly enough to evaluate. We lack God's eye for gauging fruit. Our lenses are bent with bias, and our vision is splotched with blind spots. But those who are in Christ aren't left to the strict limitations of our humanness. We have the Lord's indwelling Spirit. Yielding to His authority and affections makes no small difference in our judgment (1 Corinthians 2:12-16). When we look through spiritual eyes, we can see fruit for what it is—we can distinguish between pride and confidence, between self-abasement and humility, between contentiousness and healthy confrontation.

I am desperate for eyes that not only see but perceive (Matthew 13:14). This is one of my most frequent and heartfelt pleas in prayer. God is required on both ends of the sight spectrum. He alone can reveal what can only be perceived, and He alone can help us perceive what only He reveals.

Our spiritual eyesight, even in hindsight, will never be twenty-twenty on this side of the sky, for "now we see in a mirror dimly" (1 Corinthians 13:12). But in that dim light, if we're willing to let go of our willful blindness, God will cause us to see things a bit more clearly, like a morning fog dispelling over a hillside vineyard.

Sometimes we won't be glad about what we see. Molded, marred, or bug-scarred fruit is no welcome sight. But we will always be better off knowing. Delusion never delivers. Denial can't sweeten acrid grapes. But hard work now can produce a different crop next year.

I've been in an intense season of fog lifting. I'm sure you've experienced something similar, and perhaps the most distinguishing feature of such a season is that, in retrospect, we can't fathom how those things weren't obvious to us earlier. The signs were often right there in front of us, but what we want to believe—what we need to believe—has a strange way of swaddling the truth in a thick, cozy cloud.

We want to believe the best about people in our identity groups, and thankfully, the best is often the truth. But one reason we may want to think the best about them is because we also want to believe the best about ourselves, and no sight is quite as unsettling as fog clearing from a mirror. More often than not, those clearings coincide—about other people and ourselves. I can think of few times in my life when clarity came to me about another person and the glare of truth didn't bounce back on me. God can give sight to the blind in more ways than one.

When we come out of the fog and realize that our fruit, or the fruit of our group, is rotten, either we can face it and find a way to respond to it, or we can reinforce the cover. In this season of lifting fog, some things have become increasingly clear to me, particularly in the closest rows of the vineyard of faith where I'm planted. Mind you, I have my own vision impairments, so I'll offer these as findings rather than hard, cold facts.

- Honest disunity is better than unity in something dishonest. In honest disunity, we can at least face where we're fractured, own up to our differences, and unify around our urgent need for God. Unity at all costs, however, not only bears poor fruit, it can also bear criminal fruit and even killer fruit, excusing the inexcusable.
- Nothing is unforgivable, thank God. But some things cannot be excused. They must be repented of and dramatically corrected and permanently changed. Being loyal to people at the expense of loyalty to Christ and His gospel and to the simple truth bears a harvest of unrighteousness every time.
- Extremism bears poor fruit almost across the board, even when we think our extremes are extremely biblical. More often, upon humble reexamination, we will find that, according to Scripture, our extremes have exceeded the commands of Christ.

The beautiful part about the fog clearing on rows of rotten grapes is that we can see with our own eyes that something's gone wrong. That's what it takes, you know. As long as we're in the fog, we won't change. We can't depend on our sense of smell. It's possible to inhale a certain stench for so long that our sense of smell adapts. We have no idea how bad something stinks. But when the fog lifts and we see the bitter, mangled fruit, our eyes grow wide, and all of a sudden, our nasal airways awaken and sting.

Woe are we! What are we to do?

Sing, that's what we do. Join in the song of lament. Give way to the regret. Sorrow with the cello. Mourn and grieve, if you don't like what you see. Let the requiem's minor key wind around your heart and lead it to repentance. Weep if you will, but sing with all your might. Sing with your Beloved the song of the vineyard. Sing the fourth verse loud and clear. Open your mouth, and make the Beloved's inquiry your own.

Why did it yield wild grapes?

Why, Lord? Why did this turn out the way it did?

He knows. He tells those who listen.

To our great relief, even rotten fruit finds a place in the vineyard. In the efficient economy of cultivation, nothing is wasted.

The vinedresser does a curious thing with the rotten fruit. He turns it back into the soil and there, underground, by some spectacular organic miracle of nature, it fertilizes a future harvest.

CHAPTER 6

hills

I was raised in the hills of Arkansas, and hills are still where my soul longs to roost, even as I dwell at a nose-bleeding eighty feet above sea level near the Gulf Coast of Texas. When I was a child, my bare feet walked, skipped, and ran themselves callous all over the piney woods of Ouachita Hills.

The terrain in our quaint college town of Arkadelphia, Arkansas, might have been perfect for growing grapes, but let me assure you, there were no vineyards on our slopes. Had their usage been strictly limited to table grapes and fruit juice, even their appearance of evil would have thrown our Baptist college into the end times. No doubt the shelves at our local Piggly Wiggly would have been cleared of every last canned good, and the congregants of our First, Second, Third, Fourth, Fifth, Sixth, Seventh, Eighth, and Ninth Baptist churches would have been hurled into a fate worse than death: unity.

Clark County was dry in those days, and if you were brash enough to drink something harder than a Dr. Pepper, you would have had to drive your hell-bound self to Hot Springs to get it. As a child, based on all I'd overheard, I was pretty sure that what put the heat in Hot Springs was the scorching flame of hell itself. Drinking was the worst of sins, and drunkards, the worst of sinners.

Under the military-style headship of my father, Major Albert B. Green—who struggled, as most of us have, with considerable duplicity—we kids could do anything on earth and get away with it (and I do mean anything) except drink. This explains the rampant alcoholism that ensued.

Now please don't get antsy on me. I'm not here to debate the benefits or detriments of teetotalism. In these pages, we're after the spiritual lessons of the vinedresser, vineyard, vine, branch, grape, raisin, and wine, which are multitudinous in the Bible but tend to be handled with inordinate timidity in traditions like mine.

As we take stock of one of the most familiar metaphors in the full stretch of the sacred scrolls, our goal is to multiply our insights into the divine makings of immensely fruitful lives, not to get derailed by side conversations about wine versus grape juice.

Perhaps you feel these disclaimers need not be said. That may be the case for most of us, but I have a particular soft spot for people like me who, at twenty-five years old, would have wanted to read a book of this sort but would have done so, if at all, underneath a sheet with a flashlight.

+ + +

Whatever bewildering memories linger from my upbringing within the four teetering walls of the Green house, those Arkansas hills make up for the hard parts. Those hills will ever enchant me. In my dreams, I'm a child again, rolling horizontally down the hill outside our home, as thin as a pencil, hands bravely glued to my side and sweet gum leaves and pine needles sticking to my sweater. Meanwhile, choruses of trees sing welcome songs to autumn, and its first chilly breeze whispers, "Wandering heart, come home."

I have to believe that God has a special affinity for hills. True, some of Scripture's best scenes are captured on mountaintops, but even so, the placement of the Promised Land could lead a person to think He has a special place in his heart for a rolling terrain.

God brought His vine, Israel, out of Egypt. He escorted it the long way through the wilderness, fed it, watered it with wonders, split a river wide open to keep it from drowning, and vacuumed the riverbed dry to keep it from dragging in the mud. Then He planted it in the piece of real estate He'd prepared for it. But where, exactly, was this place He picked out?

Perhaps we know the geographical answer, but I'm pushing for something closer to a topographical answer.

Isaiah has been singing the answer to us all along, but now that the theme of his lyric has been established, it's time to start paying close attention to some of his specific words.

> *Let me sing for my beloved*
> *my love song concerning his vineyard:*
> *My beloved had a vineyard*
> *on a very fertile hill.*
> *He dug it and cleared it of stones,*
> *and planted it with choice vines.*

ISAIAH 5:1-2

Every element involved in the Beloved's preparation of the vineyard bears witness to the practices of vine growers throughout time, both in the new world and the old. We will explore each of these elements in the chapters ahead.

He chose a fertile spot.
He selected a place on a hill.
He dug it up.
He cleared it out.
He removed the stones.
He planted the vines.

If someone asked us to close our eyes and picture a rural landscape covered by vineyards, most of us would imagine a scene of rolling hills and slopes like those depicted in countless photographs and movie scenes. The most famous vineyards in the world are on high places and hills—but not for the sake of great art. They're planted there for something dramatically less poetic: drainage.

Author and gardening aficionado Jeff Cox puts it like this: "Grapes do not like wet feet."[1] I get that somehow. (I particularly don't like wet socks, although I'm hard pressed to find an analogy there.) This isn't to say that vines can't thrive on flatter acreage, particularly these days, with mechanical and chemical engineering. But flat terrain can be risky business. Standing water does to a root system what being held underwater does to a human—it deprives the plant of oxygen. Roots have to drink to survive, but they also must be able to breathe.

Some of the most breathtaking and superbly productive vineyards in Europe are planted on steep slopes. Vineyards along certain parts of the Mosel River in Germany are perched like stadium bleachers, cheering on the Rhine's glassy little sister with unabashed affection. Their vines aren't trained on conventional trellises. They are artfully rounded into heart shapes, a feast to the eyes but also a loving favor to hardworking laborers, providing simpler access for hand-tending the vines.

Since Isaiah raised the issue of placement by voicing the Beloved's choice of venue, we'll add another vocabulary word from viticulture to our study of vines and branches. A vineyard's *aspect* is a combination of two factors: the direction it faces and the degree it slopes. An aspect that faces the sun can be a remarkable boon to a vineyard in a cold climate. But a mountainside presents another problem the sun can't solve. The more drastic the incline, the greater the risk of excessive soil erosion. A little can be good but a heavy loss equals a slow death. Split the difference between valleys and steeps, and voilà! You have yourself a hill.

Like most real estate, when it comes to establishing vineyards, location is everything. Of course, God knew this all along, and He lets the reader in on the secret right there in Scripture. David writes, "The earth is the LORD's and the fullness thereof" (Psalm 24:1). In other words, God had His pick of property when He selected a vineyard. He isn't much for hemming and hawing, and He has never checked an "undecided" box on a single questionnaire in His eternal existence. He is deliberate in His choices, and the world is His oyster. By no mere accident, He chose to plant His vineyard on a hill.

By the time Moses came around, Abraham's descendants had lived in Egypt for so many generations that they couldn't have known that their cries for freedom from oppression were actually a response to a divine calling: *Wandering heart, come home.*

God is the initiator of all things in accordance with His will, and we are the respondents. God heard their cries and brought a vine out of Egypt. Then He led that vine straight for the hills.

Let Deuteronomy testify:

The land that you are entering to take possession of it is not like the land of Egypt. . . . But the land that you are going over to possess is a land of hills and valleys, which drinks water by the rain from heaven, a land that the LORD your God cares for. The eyes of the LORD your God are always upon it, from the beginning of the year to the end of the year.

DEUTERONOMY 11:10-12

Forgive the firm grasp of the obvious, but without valleys, there are no hills. You can't recognize hill country without low country. You can't adequately revere a rise without respecting the risk of a fall. In Scripture, hills and mountains are not just about altitudes. They're about action. Movement. Ups and downs. They're about ascending and descending, like angels on Jacob's ladder.

Hills require intentionality. You can't just casually walk them. You have to climb them. You engage your calves and thighs, and your legs will remind you days later that you did. You have to watch your footing on the slopes, or you'll slip.

But once you make it to the top, the panorama is your prize. For anyone with any sense, altitude changes attitude. Up there, you get a whole different perspective on where you've been and where you're going.

I don't know what your climb is like right now. Maybe your muscles are burning from the fatigue of a hard marriage or an

YOU HAVE BEEN

intentionally

PLANTED.

YOU DIDN'T LAND

HERE BY ACCIDENT.

arduous job or the scaling of a painful relationship. It seems like you've been hiking for half a lifetime already, and the worst part is that you can't even see the top.

You get to catch your breath though, you know. No one can keep up a stiff climb indefinitely without a breather. I would imagine you feel like hiding from time to time, like I do.

The psalmist saw God as his hiding place. What God was for David, He can be for us. He loves us just as much. He regards our steep challenge with equal compassion. He promises that your struggle will not be wasted, even if it feels that way now.

Perhaps Eugene Peterson's paraphrase of Psalm 31 could serve as a little oxygen to your lungs right now:

> *You're my cave to hide in,*
>   *my cliff to climb.*
> *Be my safe leader,*
>   *be my true mountain guide.*
> *Free me from hidden traps;*
>   *I want to hide in you.*
> *I've put my life in your hands.*
>   *You won't drop me,*
>   *you'll never let me down.*
>
> PSALM 31:3-5, MSG

+ + +

Hills and mountains are glorious collisions of the Creator's geometry and artistry. They own the cinematography of epic romance, posing as obstacles to be crossed by a lover who will stop at nothing to get to his beloved.

The voice of my beloved!
  Behold, he comes,
leaping over the mountains,
  bounding over the hills.
SONG OF SOLOMON 2:8

Admit that the scene wouldn't be the same if the lover described in this verse had run an equal distance at the high school track.

In the world of viticulture, the vinedresser needs endurance, education, skill, experience, intensity, passion, and timing. His skill at attending, waiting, sweating, clipping, and tasting are all on display in one productive vineyard. Valleys will do, but mountain slopes and hillsides prop up the vinedresser's handiwork like easels displaying works of Impressionist art.

Remember when Jacob, whom God renamed Israel, spoke those prophetic blessings over his twelve sons after they were reunited in Egypt, just before the old patriarch died? And remember that when he finally got to Joseph, ten sons deep, how he called him "a fruitful vine" (Genesis 49:22, CSB)?

Centuries later, God called on His servant Moses to speak prophetic blessings over the twelve tribes again. Not coincidentally, the nation was again gathered as one and was again embarking on a whole new era.

This time the direction was precisely reversed. They were returning to the land where their ancestors had been before they were uprooted and planted in Egypt's Nile-nourished soil. This time it was Moses, not Jacob, who was at the threshold of death. This time the book of Deuteronomy was drawing to an end, not the book of Genesis. This time Joseph's fruitful vine wouldn't just grow; it would propagate under the warm rays of its native sun.

Bask in the exceeding blessing over Joseph from the mouth of Moses, God's servant.

Of Joseph he said,

"Blessed by the LORD be his land,
 with the choicest gifts of heaven above,
 and of the deep that crouches beneath,
with the choicest fruits of the sun
 and the rich yield of the months,
with the finest produce of the ancient mountains
 and the abundance of the everlasting hills,
with the best gifts of the earth and its fullness
 and the favor of him who dwells in the bush.
May these rest on the head of Joseph,
 on the pate of him who is prince among his brothers."
DEUTERONOMY 33:13-16

Joseph's blessing shoots from the ground in a geyser of adjectives. *Choicest* gifts. *Choicest* fruits. *Rich* yield. *Best* gifts. The *finest* produce of the ancient mountains. The abundance of the *everlasting* hills. Spectacular aspects, complete with solar panels.

The prize still goes to the boy with the multicolored coat. Is it any wonder at all that he required extra humbling?

No one in Moses' original audience with a working ear would have missed his reference to "the favor of him who dwells in the bush." The New International Version makes the connection even plainer: "the favor of him who dwelt in the *burning* bush" (Deuteronomy 33:16, emphasis added).

Only one individual among the hundreds of thousands gathered on the plains of Moab that day had ever seen the manifestation of God dwelling in the burning bush. Moses would not be permitted to cross over into the Promised Land, but the One who'd called him on the backside of a desert would bury him on top of a mountain with a perfect panoramic view.

No tribe of Israel would carry Joseph's name. His sons, Ephraim and Manasseh, would be the tribal ancestors instead. Joseph's vine was never meant for boundaries anyway. As his father, Jacob, had prophesied four centuries earlier,

> *Joseph is a fruitful vine,*
>   *a fruitful vine near a spring,*
>   *whose branches climb over a wall.*

GENESIS 49:22, NIV

The vine that God brought out of Egypt and into the Promised Land originally grew—not perfectly, but pleasingly—and spread over the hills and down through the valleys (Deuteronomy 11:11). But in Isaiah's song to his Beloved, the prophet croons poetically not of multiple hills but of a singular hill, symbolic of the whole land, where God planted His vineyard: "My beloved had a vineyard on a very fertile hill."

When the audience in the mid-eighth century BC heard Isaiah's song, they knew exactly which hill the lyric conveyed. Had they reserved room for any doubt, the Beloved removed it when He addressed the hill directly two verses later:

> *My beloved had a vineyard*
>   *on a very fertile hill. . . .*
> *And now, O inhabitants of Jerusalem*
>   *and men of Judah,*
> *judge between me and my vineyard.*

What more was there to do for my vineyard,
that I have not done in it?

ISAIAH 5:1-4

Five chapters later, the prophet Isaiah connects the dots with a permanent marker in his reference to "the mount of the daughter of Zion, the hill of Jerusalem" (Isaiah 10:32). In other words, God planted His beloved vine on the hilly city of Jerusalem.

Fast-forward seven more centuries, to a grassy hillside near the lapping mouth of the Sea of Galilee. Seated above His audience, where His voice would amplify, Jesus delivered the incomparable Sermon on the Mount. The words He broadcasted to His disciples have since been repeated by every generation of followers called by His name. Here are some of the most memorable lines from that sermon:

You are the light of the world. A city set on a hill cannot
be hidden.

MATTHEW 5:14

Jesus left the identity of the city in question wide open. There is no definite article preceding that noun. While He declared His followers "*the* light of the world," He described them simply "*a* city set on a hill."

The crowd was gathered nearly eighty miles north of Jerusalem on a Galilean hillside, but many a mind's eye would have conjured up a postcard of the most important city in their Jewish world. Jerusalem, after all, was

the city of our God . . . beautiful in elevation . . . the joy of
all the earth . . . the city of the great King.

PSALM 48:1-2

Every faithful pilgrim listening to Jesus preach had made the arduous journey to appear before God within Jerusalem's borders at the great feasts held there each year. If they neared her by night, she was alight with innumerable lamps. If they neared her by day, with the sun radiating from the limestone of Herod's Temple, she would have been almost blinding under a cloudless sky.

In Scripture after Scripture, only one direction is given to the city of Jerusalem (also referred to as Zion), no matter where the pilgrim's journey began: "*up* to Jerusalem." Everything was downhill from there.

+ + +

You, too, have been intentionally planted. You didn't land here by accident. The direction you face, the way your life slopes—none of it came about by happenstance. There may be days when you grow weary of climbing and you long for flatter terrain. But the slopes are overlaid with tremendous purpose. God uses them to tilt us toward the light, to drain the sludge from our hearts with spring rains, and to offer us a view of the landscape that will one day turn into vision.

CHAPTER 7

rocks

As you may recall from the introduction, my grape crush began in a taxi, as my daughters and I traveled from our hotel in rural Tuscany to Siena. Let me recap the late-September scene for you: grape harvesters were moving rhythmically up and down the rows on the hillside vineyard, clipping the last ripe clusters and dropping them into buckets.

The sight alone would have been sublime enough to fuel my crush, but love at first sight isn't really my pattern. Words are my love language. My crush was inked like a tattoo on my shoulder by what our cab driver said.

I know you're expecting something poignant and piercing right now, but it won't be. Our Italian driver could speak only the most basic conversational English, but what she lacked in proficiency she made up for in enthusiasm. In her gorgeously thick accent, with a movie-worthy lilt, she announced, "I love to talk to Americans! I can practice my English!"

Now, if you read those words quickly, you didn't hear her. Try it again, nice and slow, and go high and hang long on the upper-case syllables:

"i LOVE-a to talk to aMERicans! i can PRACtice my ENGlish!"

Never mind that Great Britain is a quick leg upstairs and down the hall to the left from the Italian leather boot. The raven-haired woman had three starry-eyed Americans wrapped around her little finger in five seconds flat.

Spellbound by the midmorning sight of a vineyard at harvest, I sputtered all manner of marvel and awe. She adjusted her rearview mirror to catch my gaze, and the way her brown eyes sparkled and her temples crinkled, I could tell there was some mischief in her grin. I was game.

"Would you like-a to know something about-a the grapes?" she asked.

"Oh, yes, I would. You've got a captive audience right here."

"The grapes," she said, lowering her chin and raising her brows authoritatively, "they like-a the rocky soil."

That was it—the moment I fell in love.

I'm sorry if that's anticlimactic. It's just that I've never managed in all these years to find a single bucket of soil within a country mile of my existence that didn't have rocks clanging around in it.

I knew in that moment I'd found my fruit. It was-a the grape.

Before night fell that evening, I'd hit the research engine. By the time our plane hit the tarmac in Houston a week later, I had an order underway for an eighteen-inch stack of books on viticulture. Within a few weeks, I'd read most of them from cover to cover and was on the hunt for more.

✦ ✦ ✦

Having surveyed hills in the previous chapter, we have now arrived at the time to take the shovel to them.

My beloved had a vineyard
  on a very fertile hill.
He dug it and cleared it of stones,
  and planted it with choice vines.
ISAIAH 5:1-2

The precise order of preparations for the vineyard in Isaiah's song is quite telling. But without a word of advice from experienced vinedressers, amateur viticulturists (like most of us) would instinctively reverse the first two actions.

The way I picture the process, the landowner would pick out the perfect hill and then clear it of stones scattered on the surface. Only then, once the land was free of the obstacles, would the vinedresser start taking the shovel to the earth and turning over the soil.

However, the order in the Beloved's song is reversed. He dug it and *then* cleared it of stones.

Isaiah's order of events here communicates one of the prime draws of the particular property the Beloved chose, driving us right to the characteristic of the vitis vinifera, the common grapevine, that first swept me off my feet. After doing some digging in my new viticulture library, I discovered that our cabdriver was right on target. "All grapes have an affection for gravel, flint, slate, or stony soils, and the best acres are so infertile and stony that a corn farmer wouldn't take them as a gift."[1]

See what this is saying? What's fertile for a vine might be fatal for corn.

The author goes on to explain that rocks aren't simply obstacles

WITH GOD,
nothing HAS A
HAPHAZARD END,
NO MATTER HOW
CHAOTIC THE
MEANS MAY
SEEM.

the vinedresser has to contend with; they're something the grapes *require* in order to thrive.

> In Bordeaux, Château Ducru-Beaucaillou is so named
> because of its "beautiful pebbles." Graves, the great region
> to the south of Bordeaux, takes its name from the French
> word for gravel. Good California grape soils are flecked
> with flint, obsidian, and volcanic debris.[2]

British author Jamie Goode has an insatiable passion for the fruit of the vine. He holds a PhD in plant biology, bringing expertise alongside his years of experience to the banqueting table. Best of all, he writes about grapes with a sense of familiarity—like he knows them personally.

> Making the vines struggle generally results in better
> quality grapes. It's a bit like people. Place someone in a
> near-perfect environment, giving them every comfort
> and all that they could ever want to satisfy their physical
> needs, and it could have rather disastrous consequences
> for their personality and physique. If you take a grapevine
> and make its physical requirements for water and
> nutrients easily accessible, then (somewhat counter-
> intuitively) it will give you poor grapes.[3]

Goode goes on to say that good soil gives the grapevine a choice—and given the choice, it will opt for the easy way instead of going to the trouble of bearing fruit.

[Give the grapevine] a favourable environment and it
will choose to take the vegetative route: that is, it will put
its energies into making leaves and shoots. Effectively,
it is saying, "This is a fine spot, I'm going to make
myself at home here." It won't be too bothered about
making grapes. But make things difficult for the vine, by
restricting water supply, making nutrients scarce, pruning
it hard and crowding it with close neighbours, and it will
take the hump. It will sense that this is not the ideal place
to be a grapevine. Instead of devoting itself to growing big
and sprawling, it will focus its effort on reproducing itself
sexually, which for a vine means making grapes.[4]

In other words, as long as the grape plant is feeling comfortable
and unchallenged, she will gleefully leaf. She will award leaves,
leaves, and leaves upon leaves to her sweet-natured host. She will
bear wreaths of leaves to her happy heart's content. Eventually
she will become so thick with leaves that the hungry passerby will
observe, "There's nary a cluster to eat."

The grape plant reproduces when she gets concerned that her
survival is at risk. She responds to the threat by doing her best to
ensure that her kind makes it even if she doesn't.

The next time you throw a plump, ripe grape into your mouth,
thank its sacrificial mother, who feared she wouldn't make it
through the pregnancy.

✦   ✦   ✦

Those who fear being irreparably scandalized by becoming privy
to the reproductive habits of the grapevine may want to skip
this paragraph, but I include it because it lends itself to a certain
amount of application. Cultivated vines, with rare exceptions, are

hermaphroditic. They possess the reproductive organs of both the male and the female.[5]

A full development of the metaphor is obviously fraught. Here's what should go without question, however: both male and female have been purposed to be present in the work of the divine Vinedresser. We are each called, male and female alike, to be part of the Vine's cultivar, or purposefully cultivated variety (Genesis 1:27). From the very start, Jesus called both men and women to His gospel work. God poured out His spirit on His sons and His daughters, and He wastes no willing life (Acts 2:18).

This fruitfulness is born of the Spirit, of course, and not of the flesh. In God's vineyard, flowering that turns to fruit does not occur by fertilization between male and female—we're not talking about Christian men and women getting married and having children. The ability to produce immense fruit comes solely from the life force of the Vine.

John 15 depicts a kind of fruit-bearing that Christ prizes above all others. Every life that's attached to Him possesses the supernatural capacity to be stupendously productive. Like the natural grape plant, however, we might be inclined to wonder sometimes whether the ground where we're planted is trying to cultivate us or kill us.

Welcome to the fruitful vineyard, where grapes grow only in tension.

If the grape plant's sunshiny field isn't rocky enough, she'll be all showy, with lush green leaves, but bear little fruit. If the grape plant's field is too rocky, she'll lack enough earth for hearty roots and mournfully shrivel up. Thus, the landowner looking for the perfect place to plant a choice vine does precisely what the Beloved did in Isaiah 5. He looked for a great spot in a decent climate with generous access to sun, an aspect that could soak in water but also drain it, and the right amount of rocks to make things just challenging enough for his vines to be a little uncomfortable.

The Beloved in Isaiah's song took the shovel and broke up the field to loosen and aerate the soil, but He also performed the task of turning up stones that couldn't be seen from the surface. In doing so, He could survey His ratio of soil to rocks and start sorting.

On the hill of all hills that the Beloved chose, the brand of rock was undoubtedly limestone. It's as native to Israel as salt is to the sea. It's such a central feature in the city of Zion that it earned itself the name "Jerusalem stone." Throughout the city's history, limestone has been quarried for the construction of the city's most famous structures.

More to the point, the limestone prevalent in the soil would have played benefactor to the grapevine in Isaiah's song in impressive ways.

First, it would have been a primary contributor to the hill's rich *terra rossa* (red clay-like soil).

Second, the small outcroppings broken up in the soil would have helped the roots breathe and drink, in addition to providing adequate stress for the vine to make grapes.

Third, rocks cleared from the field were perfect for being repurposed as walls around the vineyard. These walls would deter animals such as jackals from destroying the vines. Solomon made famous one of the most unwelcome tourists in a vineyard:

> *Catch the foxes for us,*
> *the little foxes*
> *that spoil the vineyards,*
> *for our vineyards are in blossom.*
> SONG OF SOLOMON 2:15

Fourth, grape presses and vats—absolute necessities for any vineyard—would have been hewn from the most imposing, least transportable of the solid stones.

Fifth, limestone would have been put to use by the personally invested landowner to construct a watchtower for optimum care and eyes-on protection. This would be the extra mile—somewhat like an owner of an apartment complex who, at his own expense, doesn't just supply a wall and a gate for a building but also hires an on-site security guard.

> *He dug it and cleared it of stones,*
>   *and planted it with choice vines;*
> *he built a watchtower in the midst of it,*
>   *and hewed out a wine vat in it.*
>
> ISAIAH 5:2

No wonder the Beloved could say to His vineyard, in effect, "What more could I have done for you?"

This is a pretty impressive list of perks—necessities, even—that come out of the same stubborn rocks we assume are out to get us. In the hands of an able Vinedresser, rocks aren't just something to stub our toe on. They're catalysts for our growth.

Still, from where we sit, even on this side of the Cross, where death gives way to life, sometimes what God has done *for* us can feel, instead, like something He has done *to* us.

+ + +

I've never warmed up to my rocky soil. Even after a lifetime of practice, I'd still throw out every outcropping and sift out every pebble if I could. If I had my way, I'd mix the perfect soil for myself, comfy and cozy—and, for crying out loud, clean. I'd do the same for my loved ones. To be perfectly honest, it's embarrassing how long this rocky soil has lasted.

Sometimes, when I look at the faces around me, I can almost read the unspoken questions. Maybe I'm imagining things, but here's what I wonder if they're thinking:

Can't you people get it together any better than this?
Apparently not.
Your family is still dealing with that?
Apparently so.

I look around at other servants, and at least from what I can tell, some of them don't seem to have interminable drama. True, a few do, and God help me, sometimes I catch my foolish self wondering about them what others must wonder about my family and me. *What's gone wrong over there? And why doesn't it get fixed?*

For the life of me, I cannot get my life to fix. Oh, I've tried, all right. If effort could ease the way, I'd be walking on a carpet of marshmallows. Still, challenges in my life never cease to loom large. Sometimes they loom so large they nearly eclipse the sun. With a sketchy background like mine, the simplest explanation is that I sinned so grievously and made so many foolish choices, I sabotaged the rest of my life beyond recovery. But that doesn't sound much like the gospel of Jesus, does it? "You're completely forgiven, slate wiped clean, but, wow, there's nothing I can do about this mess you made."

Sixty years in, I have a feeling the rocky soil in the life of the Jesus follower is not so much about failure as it is about fruitfulness. I think one of these days, after we've seen Christ face-to-face, He may get around to saying something like, "Remember all those hard things I grew you through? I did you a favor. You can thank

Me now." And I bet we will, and on that side of things, I bet we'll mean it.

Oh, but I want it to be easier. Don't you? Aren't we all like Peter, who after being told of uncontrollable difficulties ahead, pointed John's direction and asked, "Lord, what about him?"

"What is that to you?" He answered. "You must follow me" (John 21:21-22, NIV).

I can't explain why the soil of some tremendously fruitful lives doesn't seem to be as stone prone, but I'm pretty sure Jesus thinks that's none of my business.

Our part is to follow Jesus. He knows what He's doing with you. No one's loved more than you. No one's a bigger priority than you. No one else is so high on His list of favorites that your contribution to the body of Christ is drowned out or diminished.

In fact, God doesn't play favorites. Paul made this spectacularly clear when he wrote about "those who seemed to be influential," saying "what they were makes no difference to me; God shows no partiality" (Galatians 2:6). Then in Colossians 3:24-25, he says, "You are serving the Lord Christ . . . and there is no partiality." Yet again in Ephesians 6:9, he says, "There is no partiality with him."

I want to take a moment to point out here that there are good rocks and bad rocks. Some rocks in our lives are part of the native soil and are used by God to challenge us and help us grow. But there are other kinds of rocks that are part of a noxious system—non-native rocks that are intended to crush all life and goodness.

Rocks like this might include abuse. Or being forced to serve as someone else's collateral damage. Or being pressured to "take one for the team," which actually means "Let us sin against you and don't tell anyone." Jesus sees all this. He knows when the stones near your feet first bruised your flesh and when they were thrown at you intentionally by others.

Oh, He knows, all right. Some rocks we should not hesitate to ask Him to move on our behalf. They aren't remotely native to God's soil. They come from the hands of the devil. When they're thrown at us, we don't sit back and just take it. We seek safety and tell about it. We seek counsel and healthy community to help us clear them out. Those rocks are too big and too dangerous to be lifted alone.

If you never seem to escape the rocks for long in your day in, day out living, know that you are not alone. There are many others of us who make our homes in the rocky soil.

My most meaningful work has come out of the meanest of seasons:

> Every major book I've written was composed under circumstances that felt an eighth of an inch from unbearable. Not one time has writing a book come easily for me.
> I have been in poor shape for my prime opportunities so often that it's uncanny to the point of comical.
> If I'm doing well, someone right next to me—someone dear and near to my heart—is not.
> Most of the time, something somewhere on this body hurts.
> The times when I'm in my best possible mood for public speaking, I'm the most prone to say something profoundly asinine.
> For me, winning is only having to spend about 10 percent of my time saying I'm sorry.
> Whenever I have a small window of opportunity to feel proud of myself, I stand in front of it like Rose at the nose of the *Titanic*, but just as I feel the wind in my face, a tornado comes out of nowhere and blows me to Kingdom come.
> Fairy tales never work out for me.

This is how my life has transpired much of the time. Don't let me convince you that I walk a road of constant suffering. Not only would that be untrue, it would be an insult to those who actually do. Like most people, I have journeyed through legitimate seasons of suffering, and those seasons find a vital place in fruit bearing.

At the moment, the soil beneath my feet has its share of rocks. Not boulders, perhaps, but rocks nonetheless. I can still walk just fine, but the soles of my feet remain a bit stone-bruised.

Whether you find yourself in a tumultuous season or a season of relative calm, the vineyard has much to teach us about dealing with rocky soil. The Beloved is faithful to clear out many stones, but there are others He may put to use.

I did you a favor. You can thank Me now.

The favor is dependency. We who have never stopped wanting Jesus have likely never stopped needing Jesus. And if our passion waned for a brief while, we were always only one crisis from the next revival.

God is sovereign. He can do what He pleases with each of His servants. But what He cannot do is act against His character. He cannot sin against us. He cannot shut off His heart toward us. He cannot be unbiased toward us. He cannot treat us like we don't belong to Him.

> *He does not deal with us according to our sins,*
> > *nor repay us according to our iniquities.*
> *For as high as the heavens are above the earth,*
> > *so great is his steadfast love toward those who fear him;*
> *as far as the east is from the west,*
> > *so far does he remove our transgressions from us.*
> *As a father shows compassion to his children,*
> > *so the LORD shows compassion to those who fear him.*

For he knows our frame;
 he remembers that we are dust.

PSALM 103:10-14

Dust in His hands.

Clay.

Soil.

He keeps shaping and reshaping us from glory to glory, and when living becomes nearly the death of us, He leans over our clay bodies and breathes fresh life into our lungs.

Sometimes I can reason like this—peacefully, sensibly, with wonder and awe and even tearful gratitude that God would be so kind to entrust me with difficulties. Other times all I can say is, "What the heck?"

Isaiah 46:10 conveys something about God's omniscience that gives me comfort almost every time. He knows the end from the beginning. The mind of God knows no bounds. What is true of His knowledge in universal matters is true of His knowledge in our human matters.

We are, after all, His treasures. He knows His aim with each of our lives. We are arrows in His hand, and He knows where to land us. He knows precisely what He desires to accomplish in us. With Him, nothing has a haphazard end, no matter how chaotic the means may seem.

I'm no mind reader, but I have a hunch about the answer to one of your biggest questions.

What the heck?

The Gardener is setting you up for a bushel of fruit.

PART 3

The Vine

I am the vine; you are the branches.
Whoever abides in me and I in him,
he it is that bears much fruit.

JOHN 15:5

vine

The disciples expected a regular Passover meal—a special occasion, to be sure, but it was nothing if not predictable. They knew every part of the meal, both script and song, by heart. They'd observed the feast with their kin every year of their lives. Long gone was the haste with which the original participants ate (Exodus 12).

Now rememberers reclined and settled in for the hours long retelling of the Exodus story. The slow recollection transported the imaginations of diners around the table to that fateful night in Egypt, when the Hebrew people swathed their doorposts in lamb's blood so the Lord would pass over their dwellings and spare the lives of their firstborns. Listeners were meant to feel the angst, for without it, how could they appreciate the relief?

Symbolic reenactments at the table escorted in a wide range of emotions:

From the bitterness of oppression and the exhaustion of
    backbreaking labor . . .

to hope deferred by Pharaoh's hardened heart . . .

to the horror of the cries of the grieving . . .

to the exultation of liberation . . .

and finally to the exaltation of Israel's Deliverer, the coming
Messiah.

The meal traditionally drew to a close with expressions of jubilant expectation of the Deliverer to come. Passover was a bloody story, but a stunning one nonetheless. Oppressors don't let go of the powerless without a fight. Too much profit is at stake.

Was the story too much for the kids? Too PG-13? Not only were the children present at the table, with all their chaos in tow; they were the intended audience and inquirers.

> *You shall observe this rite as a statute for you and for your sons forever. And when you come to the land that the LORD will give you, as he has promised, you shall keep this service. And when your children say to you, "What do you mean by this service?" you shall say . . .*
>
> EXODUS 12:24-27

The core question driving the retelling of the Exodus narrative was vocalized by the youngest person present who was capable of engaging: "Why is tonight different from all other nights?"[1]

That particular evening, in that particular setting, there were no toddlers crawling under the Passover table eating God knows what. There were no three-year-olds knocking over parents' goblets or children asking a constant stream of questions. There were the Twelve and Jesus. Oh, and there was singing. For certain, there was singing.

The question that would arise in the minds of the Twelve on that particular evening likely wasn't "Why is tonight different from all other nights?" Far more plausibly, it was "Why is tonight different from all other Passover nights?"

For starters, their meeting place was determined in a most curious way.

> *Then came the day of Unleavened Bread, on which the Passover lamb had to be sacrificed. So Jesus sent Peter and John, saying, "Go and prepare the Passover for us, that we may eat it." They said to him, "Where will you have us prepare it?" He said to them, "Behold, when you have entered the city, a man carrying a jar of water will meet you. Follow him into the house that he enters and tell the master of the house, 'The Teacher says to you, Where is the guest room, where I may eat the Passover with my disciples?' And he will show you a large upper room furnished; prepare it there." And they went and found it just as he had told them, and they prepared the Passover.*
>
> LUKE 22:7-13

For the life of me, I cannot think of any reason for Jesus to reveal the venue to Peter and John so mysteriously except for the pure adventure of it. Only a man who loved His flock more than His own flesh could have seen to such pleasures on a day He knew would end in uproarious pain.

They'd barely unwound and relaxed when Jesus said, "I have eagerly desired to eat this Passover with you before I suffer. For I tell you, I will not eat it again until it finds fulfillment in the kingdom of God" (Luke 22:15-16, NIV).

Eagerly desired. Emotive words in English, but even more so in Greek. In the original language, Jesus' words have what scholars call a "double construction"—His statement literally translates "with desire I have desired." His listeners would have known not only by the earnest look in His eyes but also by His emphatic word choice the depth of His feelings.[2]

Somewhere deep inside, I think many of us believe Jesus spends time in our company primarily out of obligation, as if we're an annoying, misfit appendage He's stuck with. After all, He promised to be with us always. He has to be true to His word. It's easy to get it in our heads that we're tolerated more than enjoyed. My guess is that most of us wouldn't picture Him *eagerly desiring* to spend time with us, yet that's precisely what Scripture says of His final evening before death. What He wanted most of all was to share a meal with His followers.

Jesus had obviously counted the days until Passover. Perhaps the hours. Perhaps the minutes. Then why bring up suffering before supper was cold? Perhaps the Twelve hardly noticed, since the next words out of His mouth suggested the Kingdom could be established before the very next Passover.

> *He took a cup, and when he had given thanks he said, "Take this, and divide it among yourselves. For I tell you that from now on I will not drink of the fruit of the vine until the kingdom of God comes."*
>
> LUKE 22:17-18

When the meaning is unclear, we tend to hear what we want to hear. If I'd been at the table that night, I'd want to hear that Jesus was staying and never leaving, and that His Kingdom was coming with no Cross or crown of thorns. I'd want to believe that by suffering, Jesus meant something philosophical, not so gruesomely physical. I'd want to hear that we all had a promotion coming—that things were starting to pay off in this upside-down world where fishers caught men and tax collectors fled their money tables to follow a King dressed like a peasant. But all my wanting wouldn't make it true.

After Jesus had passed around the cup, He picked up the bread, thanked God for it, broke it, and distributed it among the Twelve. Then He spoke these words: "This is my body, which is given for you. Do this in remembrance of me" (Luke 22:19).

Maybe the disciples had better manners than most, so perhaps they said nothing out loud. But I have to wonder if anyone at the table was thinking, *Man, why aren't you sticking with the script?*

> *Likewise the cup after they had eaten, saying, "This cup that*
> *is poured out for you is the new covenant in my blood.*
> LUKE 22:20

No one at that table knew the script better than Jesus. For the love of God, He *wrote* the script, and He would both fulfill it and finish it. The rest of the evening was not only unlike any other Passover night; it was unlike any other night in history. It was forever planned to be.

That evening the disciples were unwittingly seated at the table with "the Lamb who was slain from the creation of the world" (Revelation 13:8, NIV). The moment He breathed a soul into Adam, the Fall was inevitable and the Cross was as good as done. It was all forethought. No afterthought.

Take, drink.

Take, eat.

I often wonder how I would have responded if I'd been sitting

SO OFTEN I MISS
THE NEW THING

BECAUSE I THINK
I KNOW HOW LIFE
SHOULD GO.

around that table with Jesus on the night before He was crucified. Would I have seen the pain in His eyes? Would I have sensed the weight of what was about to unfold? Or would I have been too distracted by the fact that Jesus was going off script?

God alone knows how often I miss the new thing He's doing because I think I know how life should go. Truth be told, I don't want this night to be unlike any other night. I want to know what to expect. I want to find a good groove and have God stick to it. I forget that as the Author, He has the right to take the script on any twists and turns He desires. He alone knows how the story line has to go to reach its appointed objective. He alone knows what chapter He's on and how close He is to the finish.

+ + +

Had the disciples comprehended the significance of the unfolding revelation at the table that evening, they would have saved themselves the embarrassment of arguing over who was the greatest. One mention from Christ's lips that a betrayer was in their midst, and suddenly they were like little boys throwing on capes, competing like superheroes.

Later that night Jesus said, "You will all fall away, for it is written, 'I will strike the shepherd, and the sheep will be scattered'" (Mark 14:27).

In John's Gospel, the curtain rises on the Last Supper with Jesus getting up from the table and removing His outer robe. He wraps a towel around His waist, pours water into a basin, sets it on the floor, gets down on his knees, and starts washing their grimy feet. The irony that Judas would soon hurry from the room to betray Jesus on a pair of feet Jesus had just washed is remarkable. He was still wet between the toes when he betrayed Him.

He immediately went out. And it was night.

JOHN 13:30

"Why is this night different than all other nights?" No night had ever been so dark. The full stretch of Christ's words recorded in John 14–17, known as the "farewell discourse," occurred before Jesus went out with His disciples to the garden (John 18:1).

In an astonishing body of teaching exceeding the length of the Sermon on the Mount, Christ delivered words with the weight of the world. He promised to prepare a place for His followers in His own Father's house. Many rooms, many followers.

I don't know if we'll get our own rooms or not, but it won't matter. We'll get along better then. Jesus also declared Himself peerless, nailing down an "I am" statement that Christianity either hangs its hat on or loses its head over: "I am the way, and the truth, and the life. No one comes to the Father except through me" (John 14:6).

Jesus promised to send His followers the Holy Spirit—His very own Spirit. He called them to obedience as an outward expression of their love for Him and promised to manifest Himself to them. He warned them about trouble to come and joys that would follow anguish. In the most sublime prayer ever recorded in Scripture, He interceded for them and for those who would follow in their footsteps.

Within the same farewell discourse, Jesus also delivered the words that preoccupy us in these pages:

I am the true vine, and my Father is the vinedresser. . . .
Abide in me, and I in you. As the branch cannot bear
fruit by itself, unless it abides in the vine, neither can you,
unless you abide in me. I am the vine; you are the branches.

*Whoever abides in me and I in him, he it is that bears much
fruit, for apart from me you can do nothing. . . . By this my
Father is glorified, that you bear much fruit and so prove to
be my disciples. . . . You did not choose me, but I chose you
and appointed you that you should go and bear fruit and
that your fruit should abide.*

JOHN 15:1, 4-5, 8, 16

"I am the true vine." This is the seventh and final "I am" dec-
laration in the Gospel of John. Call it an allegory, call it a parable,
or call it a metaphor, but whatever you do, call it distinct. It's a
stand-alone in the discourse. It isn't introduced by the words "The
kingdom of heaven is like . . ." It is not future oriented. It is present
and permanent. Perhaps most importantly, it is definitive. It leaves
no room for ambiguity.

*This is what my Father is, this is what I am, and this is what
you are.*

The timing of Christ's teaching on the vine is especially compelling, because the disciples were on the move when He delivered
this message, headed to Gethsemane, the place where Jesus would
sweat blood in prayer and ultimately be arrested.

John 14 concludes with these words from Jesus to the Twelve:

*I will no longer talk much with you, for the ruler of this
world is coming. He has no claim on me, but I do as the
Father has commanded me, so that the world may know that
I love the Father. Rise, let us go from here.*

JOHN 14:30-31

The next recorded words out of His mouth? "I am the true
vine, and my Father is the vinedresser." Jesus needed no visual aid

to make His point, but His storytelling techniques in the Gospels lead us to think He was the master of show-and-tell. The "fruit of the vine" was fresh on their minds and tongues, since He'd just passed it around the table and singled it out as the symbol of "the new covenant in [His] blood."

There may have been an additional visual aid for the vine and branches, however—one that loomed large overhead as they passed the Temple on their trek to Olivet.

According to some scholars, Jesus might have paused at the Temple with His disciples after leaving the upper room, before they went to the garden of Gethsemane. At the entrance to the Holy Place in the Temple, there was a grapevine made of gold, which symbolized Israel. Commentator Gary M. Burge notes that "wealthy citizens could bring gifts to add to the vine (gold tendrils, grapes, or leaves), and these would be added by metal workers to the ever-growing vine (m. Middoth 3:8). Josephus claims that some of the grape clusters were the 'height of a man.'"[3]

In the days of Christ, the wealthy could, in effect, buy their own fruit and have it etched in gold for time immemorial. Imagine standing just below the portico of Herod's Temple, your arm draped across a child's shoulder. "See that grape up there? The extra-large one toward the top of the cluster, on the right side?" The child squints and stares, then nods his head, hoping he's fixed his eyes on the right one. "That's your grandfather's grape. And the one right below it? That's your uncle Isaac's. Make us proud and add your own one day, won't you, boy?"

He wouldn't want to tarry until old age, because that Temple would be destroyed within forty years, grapes and all.

+ + +

Sometimes it's glaringly clear in Scripture when Jesus made a revolutionary claim that flew in the face of tradition. Take the time the woman at the well brushed Him off as an amateur theologian, for instance. "When [Messiah] comes, he will tell us all things," she quipped.

His response? "I who speak to you am he" (John 4:25-26).

That kind of statement could make a woman drop her water jar and break her big toe.

Several chapters later in John's Gospel, Jesus publicly claimed to be the bread of life. When He described Himself as "the bread that comes down from heaven" that people could eat and never die, it no doubt caused an immediate stir (John 6:48-52). A rabbi didn't mess with manna and get no reaction.

Jesus' claim is no less startling here in John 15, but the gale force slips past us because we aren't first-century Israelites. We don't know what it's like to have pilgrim feet planted on the sacred ground of Jerusalem for one of the great feasts.

In Jesus' day, everybody knew what the vine represented: Israel, plain and simple. By plain, I mean obvious, not unadorned, since the prophet Hosea wrote that Israel "is a luxuriant vine that yields its fruit" (Hosea 10:1). The grapevine was so widely renowned as a symbol for Israel that it was even inscribed on coins.[4] Jesus wasn't just telling an everyday parable. He was daring to supplant Israel.

I am the true vine.
JOHN 15:1

Now the vine is not the nation. Not the land. Not the city of Jerusalem. Not the descendants of Jacob. In one fell swoop, the old vine that had been purposefully and meticulously planted by God was uprooted and summarily—and eternally—altered. There was now a new covenant. A new cup. A new vine. New wine. All in accordance with an eternal plan.

Christ's claim would have been explosive had He made it publicly. No one on the face of the earth gave more weight to land than the Israelites—and hadn't they done so because God had established this Promised Land Himself? The terroir, the sense of place, was now no place at all. It was a person—Jesus the Nazarene, of all people.

I am the true vine. This was the claim coming from the mouth of a man born in an animal shed to a girl who got pregnant outside of marriage. This time He'd stepped on ground where angels fear to tread.

A conscientious Israelite might balk, *But this is our homeland!* His response? *Now I am your homeland. Abide in Me.*

So much has needed supplanting in my life. Yours, too? All the nouns—the people, places, and things—I've believed were inseparable from who I was have been strategically targeted by God. Over the years, He has sought to supplant them with Christ alone. They weren't cast aside as worthless any more than the land was relegated to meaninglessness for the people of God. They had their role, but they simply weren't Jesus.

We struggle to imagine that God would wish to supplant the very things He Himself has supplied us. That's where this gets complicated. He'd given the Israelites the land, after all, just as He has given us our spiritual disciplines, our dreams, our visions, our vocations, our callings, and our communities of faith. So when He starts messing with those things, the earth beneath our feet starts quaking. There comes a point when the rules we've sworn by—our time-proven strategies, our five keys to victory, our twelve steps, our great habits—are no longer enough. While they're all good things, they can get entangled with Jesus Himself and start cutting off the circulation between the Vine and the branch.

He supplants only for the purpose of giving life, not taking it. He reminds us at strategic times that nothing and no one can sustain us but Him.

Jesus wants to shift your securities so that you will abide in Him alone, not in other people, places, and things. He knows that those things are bereft of the power to anchor, oxygenate, and animate you the way His Spirit does.

If you're in Christ, He is your true Vine, whether you realize it or not. But a whole new way of flourishing begins when you know it. When you count on it. When you live like it. When you let go of the vines you thought were giving you life.

Ever since that dark night that was unlike any other, that night when Jesus made His bold proclamation, each person, whether Jew or Gentile, male or female, slave or free, would be defined in relationship to a singular Vine. This Vine was no one's to own and anyone's to have.

The Vine knew it was time, though the branches took issue. Consult most any book on vineyards about when the first grapes of a new vine typically appear. You might be surprised to discover the answer.

It's year three.

CHAPTER 9

abide

The job of the branch is to abide. Fruit is assured to every branch that fulfills its singular task: abide in the Vine. "Easy," we say, and we then spend a lifetime relapsing into autonomy and then repenting, relearning what it means to abide.

In one sense, abiding sounds like the easiest command for a Jesus-follower to undertake. It means resting in the One who is stronger than we are, wiser than we are, and more powerful than we are—and who loves us and defends us. But for most of us, the not-doing is infinitely more difficult than the doing. Give us a to-do list or a deadline or an assignment, but for the love, please don't ask us to let go and be still.

This is a good time to nail down an important principle of abiding. It doesn't mean you're immobilized. That's the beauty of Christ turning this metaphor on its head. The vine, which was once the land, has now been supplanted by Christ. That means we no longer abide in a place but in a person. We reside in Jesus. When He moves, we move. When He stays, we stay.

According to Scripture, walking and abiding are not anti-thetical: "By this we may know that we are in him: whoever says he abides in him ought to walk in the same way in which he walked" (1 John 2:5-6).

At a recent conference, I got a handwritten letter I found so astonishing I had to read it three times to make sure I understood the story correctly. The woman testified to having served seventeen years of a life sentence without parole in a state penitentiary for a crime she didn't commit.

During her incarceration, she went through a stack of my in-depth Bible studies, one right after another. She said God utterly transformed her as she pored over Scripture. Her exact words? "It was like I was on a honeymoon with Jesus."

When she went through my nine-week course on the book of Esther, her heart lit up with remarkable hope. "If the king reversed Esther's death sentence, my spirit leaped believing my King of kings would reverse my death sentence."

Just think how you and I might have tried to talk her down from this impossible hope in the very likely event that God wouldn't intervene in this way. Thank goodness she didn't rely on the faith of people like me. Lo and behold, evidence surfaced that proved her innocence, and soon that sister was exonerated.

She walked out of that prison free and clear. I know she was telling the truth, because I researched the case. I've been taken for a fool before. But this was no sham. You may be thinking similar thoughts to mine: *How I wish this was everyone's story who'd ever been falsely accused.*

I want you to hear this part of her story, though, as she praised God for walking her outside those prison walls: "I'm totally free in Jesus! Even in prison, I was free."

Oh, please, take in those words again: *Even in prison, I was free.* This woman had found her abiding place, and it was Jesus. It wasn't a jail cell. It wasn't an urban apartment. It wasn't a home in the country. The withered branch had recognized its true Vine and received His life. Whether she was behind bars on a paper-thin mattress or running through a field of sunflowers, that girl was free. She'd found joy inside and joy outside because Jesus Himself was her joy, and no one could take Him away. The devil had tried to devour her, but he'd lost her forever to the Savior who had captivated her.

Once we're in Christ, the devourer can no longer feast on our souls. So he aims his efforts at the next best thing: he tries to lay waste to our effectiveness.

In our metaphor, effectiveness means fruitfulness. And what most glorifies the Father is for us to produce a profuse amount of fruit—enough to exceed natural explanation.

I am the vine; you are the branches. Whoever abides in me and I in him, he it is that bears much fruit, for apart from me you can do nothing.
JOHN 15:5

Jesus' point is not that mortal creatures are incapable of doing anything without abiding in Him. Every human is created in His image, which means we're all capable of doing good work. But image bearing and abiding are not remotely the same thing. The bodies of talented people who could not have cared less about Christ will grow cold and stiff all over the world before this day is over. Obituaries will be written and eulogies given, listing their accomplishments. All manner of works will be done by people who didn't abide in Christ for a millisecond.

The context of John 15:5 communicates something closer to this: "Apart from Me you can do nothing you couldn't do anyway." Said another way, "Apart from me, you can do nothing only I can do." John 15 is about living a naturally unexplainable life. It's about doing what we can't do on our own and becoming who we can't be on our own.

That's what attracts attention to Jesus. When weaklings become strong and timids become bold and temporal creatures do timeless work through the sheer vitality of Jesus, disproportionate fruit is produced. The fruit bearing that comes from abiding is the vintage example of a whole that is remarkably greater than the sum of its parts.

The devourer's goal is to interrupt and undercut the process of profound effectiveness. His success is not dependent upon the disciple's moral failure or loss of orthodoxy, though both tools are in his wheelhouse. We can remain surrendered to the cause of Christ, sacrificial and sanctified, gospel driven to the bone, and our fruitfulness can still suffer loss. All the devil has to do is lure us away from abiding in Christ.

To do so, he merely appeals to our natural inclination to independence and novelty.

We prefer to do things ourselves, in our own way, and if we must work in tandem with someone else, we'd prefer to find a new partner after the newness wears off. We lack the imagination to see how newness can be continually rediscovered in sameness. Give a relationship a few focused years, and we assume we know a person completely, but of course we don't. We can't. Even a finite human being has depth and breadth beyond what we could excavate in a lifetime. We rub the polishing rag over the surface so many times that we dull the skin without ever getting beneath it. Though we're multidimensional creatures, we often practice one-dimensional relationships because we are lazy by nature and because novelty requires little effort.

If human beings are host to more depth than we could mine in a lifetime, how many more layers must there be to an infinite, eternal God? We could spend every moment of life on this earth and into eternity exploring the facets of God and never get to the end of Him. That's why abiding is a lifelong quest. But something so brilliantly supernatural doesn't come naturally for us.

One of the most compelling elements of abiding is a divine curiosity to uncover more of the character and complexity of Christ. Curiosity is the far nobler sister of novelty. Curiosity invokes study. By definition, it is "interest leading to inquiry."[1] It does not look for diamonds on blades of grass; it looks for dew. If it's looking for diamonds, it mines. Curiosity isn't satisfied to climb a hill and then move on. To borrow words from Deuteronomy, it digs copper from them (Deuteronomy 8:9).

God has an undeniable affinity for progressive revelation—for peeling back the veil, inch by inch. The master of hide-and-seek, He loves to cloak the sublime with the simple.

> He grew up before him like a young plant,
>   and like a root out of dry ground;
> he had no form or majesty that we should look at him,
>   and no beauty that we should desire him.

ISAIAH 53:2

This prophecy was fulfilled by

> Christ, in whom are hidden all the treasures of wisdom and knowledge.

COLOSSIANS 2:2-3

How like the divine Concealer-Revealer to hide the very embodiment of infinite treasure beneath ordinary skin for thirty-three years. Only God could hide Christ's beauty. It's no wonder that John, the beloved disciple, dropped to the ground like a dead man when he got a glimpse of the immortal Jesus when he was exiled on Patmos (Revelation 1:17).

You need not worry that all this abiding will get boring. There's no getting used to Jesus. One of the best parts of abiding in Christ is staying close enough to catch a glimpse of what He decides to reveal.

Abide in Me. If you're willing, you'll never quit learning.

Could it be that what God loves most about His relationship with us is precisely what we do not love about it? He loves to be with us, sit with us, and walk with us. He loves to be in our company, as hard as that is for us to fathom, and to be company to us. He didn't need disciples. He could have accomplished every task He desired without them. He chose the disciples to have "part with Him" (John 13:8), to partner with Him (2 Corinthians 6:1).

God doesn't need us, either. He could accomplish all He wills from the throne of heaven. He *wants* us with Him. He longs for a relationship with us. While God desires the relational, however, we humans tend toward the transactional. "Lord, just tell me what to do and give me the power to perform it. Then let me do it." We say to the Alpha and Omega, "Give me the plan from A to Z, and leave it to me."

We forget that He came to be Immanuel, God with us.

Abide in Me. Work with Me.

+ + +

There's a scene in 1 Samuel 16 that I dearly love because it illustrates almost humorously how God reserves the right to reveal His specific leadership to His servants as we go, rather than all at once, from the start. He intends for us to stay attentive to Him—to abide in Him—rather than log in just long enough to get our download and then carry on with our business apart from Him.

The curtain rises in 1 Samuel 16 on the old prophet grieving over the colossal failure of Saul, Israel's first king. When we've worked closely with someone as their overseer or mentor and they go audaciously awry, it can be messy business to sort out their failure. Especially when we feel responsible for the way they turned out.

Samuel's own sons had not fared well. They were liars and cheaters, paid off to pervert justice. They were, in fact, the catalysts that sparked an uprising of Israel's elders to demand from Samuel no mere judge. They wanted a king (1 Samuel 8). Sometimes God gives in to our arrogant, tantrum-throwing demands to teach us a lesson. He gave them a king, all right.

Saul, son of Kish, offered the full package. He was young and wealthy, and lest we think appearance meant little to our ancestors, there was

> *not a man among the people of Israel more handsome than*
> *he. From his shoulders upward he was taller than any of*
> *the people.*
>
> 1 SAMUEL 9:2

And he was an imbecile.

When the time came for Saul to be publically proclaimed king, he was nowhere to be found. This slice of the story is golden: when they inquired of the Lord where on earth he might be, the Lord answered word for word:

> *Behold, he has hidden himself among the baggage.*
> 1 SAMUEL 10:22

Who wouldn't give their eyeteeth to hear the Lord say a thing like that?

I once watched a woman on a respectable TV variety show perform the mesmerizing talent of zipping herself up into a suitcase—a feat that took no small maneuvering. This was before hot yoga. I wondered for days what on earth made her try this in the first place. What would make a person think, out of the blue, *I believe I'll try to zip myself up in a suitcase?*

This is the kind of thing I mean by humans being multi-dimensional. You can't possibly know from the surface what makes people do what they do. That woman had more layers to her than her luggage had compartments. What made a man who was head and shoulders taller than every other Israelite crouch down behind the baggage at the time of his public presentation? Tall Man was a deep well. And this is only the beginning of his story. He'll lose his mind before this is over.

Samuel, son of Hannah, was a godly judge and a faithful prophet, and he would go to his grave as both. But in the opening of 1 Samuel 16, surely he was consumed by thoughts of his own two sons, Joel and Abijah, along with thoughts of Saul, the son of Kish. Regrets must have burned like sizzling brands on his chest, charring his flesh. Maybe Samuel had the wisdom and wherewithal not to take three strikes to mean he was out, but some of us would have found the opportunity for irresistible despair.

The LORD said to Samuel, "How long will you grieve over
Saul, since I have rejected him from being king over Israel?
Fill your horn with oil, and go. I will send you to Jesse the
Bethlehemite, for I have provided for myself a king among
his sons." And Samuel said, "How can I go? If Saul hears it,
he will kill me." And the LORD said, "Take a heifer with you
and say, 'I have come to sacrifice to the LORD.' And invite
Jesse to the sacrifice, and I will show you what you shall do."

1 SAMUEL 16:1-3

The intimacy between God and Samuel in this scene is compelling as much for its pattern as its peculiarity. Samuel seemed to
be on such familiar terms with God that not only was he able to
discern His voice, but he was willing to tell Him when His plan
sounded like it had some holes in it. The impasse was settled when
God told him, in essence, "Just take the next step. I'll show you
what to do from there."

During so much of this walk with God, we feel blindfolded.
Certain seasons are pocked with such random events that we
decide all is helter-skelter. Other seasons seem so illustriously
orchestrated that the ties between events are like streamers of spun
gold. From the very beginning, God geared the faith walk to be
relational, not informational. The latter was always intended for
the sake of the former.

We want to leap with God; He wants to walk with us. Walking
transpires step by step. It demands patience. Pacing. God's direc-
tional leading for our personal lives often unfurls in bits of light
between shadows. He says His word is a lamp to our feet, which
offers us the assurance of arm's length direction when He says, "Go."

Samuel had a smidge more than a lit-up path. He had a heifer.
I don't know this from personal experience, but it can't be all that

FOLLOWING JESUS
IS ABOUT BEING
tethered to Him
LIKE HE'S
OXYGEN.

easy to take a trip with a heifer. As the crow flies, the trip from Ramah (where Samuel was) to Bethlehem (where Jesse lived) was only about eleven miles, with Jerusalem as the halfway point. But Samuel's travelling companion was no crow. One might imagine the old prophet either growing attached to the animal or having to fight the urge to kill the stubborn thing before he ever made it to Jesse's. It's best not to romanticize obedience, especially since Samuel is long gone and we're the ones on the road from Ramah now, prone to make a pet out of our sacrifice.

Take a good, slow look at God's words to Samuel: "I will show you what you shall do."

To Abram He'd similarly said, "Go from your country . . . to the land that I will show you" (Genesis 12:1).

Lord, why can't You just tell me upon departure? Why do I have to wait for You to show me where I'm going?

Because showing requires going. It assumes presence. Accompaniment. I can send you somewhere and not go with you, but how can I show you something without being present? This same sense of connection is on display in the revelation received by the exiled apostle John.

> *I looked, and there before me was a door standing open in heaven. And the voice I had first heard speaking to me like a trumpet said, "Come up here, and I will show you what must take place after this."*
>
> REVELATION 4:1, NIV

God's interactions with Moses whisper the same relational bent: "Go, and I will be with your mouth and teach you what you shall speak" (Exodus 4:12). Check every formal translation of this verse, and you'll find the same verb: *teach*. The more predictable wording would have been, "I will *tell* you what you shall speak." But that's not what it says. *I will teach you.*

So why the emphasis on teaching instead of telling? Because teaching takes two. It requires interaction. Where there's no inter- action, there's no relationship. But make no mistake—the rela- tional arrangement Jesus presented to His followers went even beyond interaction to indwelling:

> *I am the vine; you are the branches. Whoever abides in me and I in him, he it is that bears much fruit, for apart from me you can do nothing.*
>
> JOHN 15:5

Being a branch to the true Vine means living with Christ, breath- ing with Christ, doing day-to-day life with Christ. It's the ongoing awareness of His presence, even when there's no feeling of His presence. Our lives become witness to His with-ness.

I love the way Dr. Gary M. Burge explains the mystery of abid- ing and the way it surfaces in a life.

> Christianity is not simply about believing the right things (though this is important). Nor is it simply a matter of living a Christ-like life (though this is important too). Christian experience must necessarily have a mystical, spiritual, non-quantifiable dimension. To be a disciple means having the Father, Son, and Holy Spirit living in us ([John] 14:23-26). It means having a supernatural, interior experience that is completely unlike anything available in the world. It is a way of believing (doctrine) and a way of living (ethics), but these are nurtured by the life-giving connection with Jesus Christ."[2]

In other words, following Jesus isn't just about a prescribed set of rules or a certain set of behaviors. It's about being tethered to Jesus like He's oxygen—it's about being in His presence at every moment. When you're with someone you love, it doesn't matter what you're doing; it's about doing it together.

> Today's world is not hardened in a rigid demand
> for rationalistic religious proof as it was in another
> generation. It is bona fide spiritual experience that
> authenticates religious truth in our world, and this is
> precisely what Jesus is describing. What are the outcomes
> of this sort of life? The fruit Jesus expects from the
> branches is first and foremost love. . . . This spiritual
> awakening, this transforming encounter does not always
> lead to fantastic signs and powers (though these may
> come, cf. [John] 14:12). It leads principally to a life that
> has features of Jesus' life running through its veins."[3]

Did you catch that? Abiding inevitably leads to love. A life that is lived in intimacy with Jesus is a life that is lived in love.

+ + +

Abounding in love is possible only when we abide in Him. We can't do the works of Christ by human might or by earthly power; we can only do them with the heart of Christ. We produce fruit by His Spirit alone. When you begin to feel lifeless in Him, look for the tourniquet that's cutting off the life flow. Most often we'll find it in earthly ties that are cinched too tightly.

We're meant to have the closest of loves and relationships with other people, but we can become so tightly wound up in them that the life force of Christ is reduced to an occasional random drip. The irony is that the relationships we've prioritized over Christ have been cut off from the very force that's capable of making them flourish. To cheat people of Christ in you is to cheat people of a love that breaks through the narrow confines of our natural heart.

According to one Bible commentator, the Greek word translated "branch" in John 15 "emphasizes the ideas of *tenderness* and *flexibility*."[4]

Tenderness.

Flexibility.

Sometimes when I want a Bible study group to get ridiculously excited with me over the definition of a Greek word, God rattles me with reminders that some of us are trying to survive another day of a difficult marriage, a chemo treatment, a bankruptcy, an intolerable job, parenting three kids under the age of five, or sobriety after decades of addiction. We're looking for help and hope a heck of a lot more than a Greek definition.

Part of abiding with Christ means abiding with other people, too. We are here to help people in Jesus' name. This seems elementary, as if it should go without saying, but somehow I have to say it to myself continually. When we feel like people are finally about to drive us entirely over the edge, we are in precisely the right shape for a deep breath and a momentary break. Then it's time to bear in mind once again that people are the point. They need our tenderness. They need our flexibility. They may just need us to sit with them, to abide with them.

At the risk of oversimplification, maybe abiding doesn't require deep analysis. Perhaps all I need to ask myself at the moment is whether or not I am still tender. Still flexible. At times I am neither. The branch that snaps easily is either dead or stuck in a long-past winter.

Jesus is our singular place of abiding, the terroir of every true branch. The former vine, Israel, was rooted in the land, but Jesus didn't call His disciples to cling to the land. He called them to cling to Him, even as they went to the far-flung corners of the earth.

> *Go therefore and make disciples of all nations, baptizing them in the name of the Father and of the Son and of the Holy Spirit, teaching them to observe all that I have commanded you. And behold, I am with you always, to the end of the age.*
> MATTHEW 28:19-20

With Jesus came the echoes of a new Genesis:

> *Be fruitful and multiply and fill the earth.*
> GENESIS 1:28

> *Abide in me.*
> JOHN 15:4

> *Go . . . [to] all nations.*
> MATTHEW 28:19

Stay . . . and go.

Jesus is our staying power in all our going. If you'll stay while you go, you may not always know where you're going. But you can know that wherever you end up, He will walk you there.

CHAPTER 10

pruning

Growing can look a lot like shrinking.

Sometimes you may not have the faintest clue God is busily making you more productive, because what seems far clearer is that He is intent on killing you. Perhaps the mystery is solved sooner rather than later by an increased harvest within a year or two. When this happens, fire up the grill and celebrate to the hilt, because the next time the only way you may know God wasn't killing you is that a good many years later, you're still not dead.

You'd think a branch would know whether or not it was bearing good fruit, but the branch deciphers "good" in terms of quantity alone. To the branch, the heavier the grapes, the better the harvest.

That's not how the vinedresser sees it.

The vinedresser has a name for dealing with the discrepancy between quantity and quality: pruning. My dislike for the term *pruning* predates any creditable knowledge concerning the brutal shears of basic gardening. It stems from the fact that I have an aversion to the word *prune* and lack the maturity to dissociate it. It goes like this: the word *pruning* reminds me of prunes. Prunes remind me of the elderly. The elderly remind me that I am teetering on the precipice and could be mere seconds from trading sparkling water for prune juice.

But pruning is precisely what gardeners have termed the process for generations and what Christ Himself apparently calls it when He speaks English Standard Version. Easy for Him to say— He's up there never aging. Still, pruning it is. There's no sense arguing with Him.

Nothing is more painful to the branch than pruning—and nothing is more irresponsible for the vinedresser than avoiding it.

+ + +

Pruning season occurs primarily during winter months, when limbs are leafless and dormant. The vinedresser typically pulls out his shears just before bud break, which feels like the worst possible time to the branch. This timing could lead the branch to believe that the gardener is anxious to bring to an end what already appears half-dead.

Of course, the branch could not be more mistaken. The branch is very much alive and never more poised for fruitfulness than in the wake of winter.

We know how the grapevine feels. We've been there—on the cusp of something fresh and wonderful, only to have our starry-eyed love dampened, our awakened passion quenched, our budding victory vanquished. This kind of trimming feels unjust— cruel, even.

You can see the budding. It's right there before your eyes. You can taste the breakthrough on the tip of your tongue. But just before it comes to fruition—faith made sight—your breakthrough ends up looking suspiciously more like a breakdown.

What you must trust in these moments is that anything God breaks down is intended to build you up. Anything He cuts off is to give breathing space to what He's adding on. Sometimes it's too soon to come to full bloom.

I'll leave this between you and Jesus and not presume to make a rule of it, but I think much of the time we realize later why the wait was wise. The bud was a glimpse, not a grape. But even a glimpse is a form of vision.

The gardener who will not subject his branches to pruning is not merciful. He is murderous—slowly, yes, but surely. He will first kill the quality, then the flavor, and finally the fruit itself. This is suffocation by overcrowding, or what the experts call "overcropping."

> Overcropping in a given year reduces the fruitfulness of buds in the subsequent year. So the best way to guarantee that your vines produce adequately year after year is to prune them properly year after year. . . . An unpruned vine will have from 10 to 100 times the buds necessary for a good crop of quality grapes. The vine struggles for quantity, thus maximizing its chances to reproduce. The vintner struggles for quality, maximizing his or her chances for *vin parfait*.[1]

We dwell in an age of aesthetics, where beauty is chief among aims. The purpose of the branch, however, is not the beauty of a painter's canvas—a well-tended vine covered in leaves misty with dew, filtered through the light of dawn. No, the purpose of the branch is benefit, and its benefit is found in its fruitfulness. The gardener's shears cut away a future of increasing uselessness.

Pruning, according to Jesus, is a really good sign. It doesn't just signal future fruit. It's proof of previous fruit.

Every branch in me that does not bear fruit [the vinedresser]
takes away, and every branch that does bear fruit he prunes.
JOHN 15:2

The vinedresser doesn't bother pruning branches that don't bear fruit. He prunes those that do. Receiving a cutback for impressive production is counterintuitive to us mortals, particularly in a screen-driven world where the bigger the bytes, the better the product. God, however, doesn't appear to mind being misunderstood. His determination to do us good is undeterred by accusations that He's doing us harm. He rarely takes up for Himself, since there's no place further up for Him to go. Instead, He's content to reply with the foreign language of shears in choppy syllables.

John 15 paints the picture of a vinedresser painstakingly devoted to our progress:

Bear fruit (verse 2).
Bear more fruit (verse 2).
Bear much fruit (verse 8).

No one loses. As Christ puts it, here are the benefits of pruning:

My Father is glorified (verse 8).
You prove to be my disciples (verse 8).
My joy may be in you, and your joy may be full (verse 11).

It may take a while for joy to come in the midst of pruning, but it is inevitable. Fruitfulness is always finally felicity.

God, Creator of shrub and tree, who planted and landscaped Eden, has intimate knowledge of the health of every branch and the potential of every bud on His vine. While "every branch that does bear fruit he prunes" (John 15:2), the way He prunes each is His call entirely.

He controls the metaphor in John 15; the metaphor does not control Him. That means He can get creative with His shears. But I'll tell you what God can't do: He can't do evil. He can't be unloving, because He Himself is love. His goodness is inseparable from His glory (Exodus 33:18-19). So you can believe, as David did, that you will see the goodness of the Lord in the land of the living (Psalm 27:13).

+ + +

For some of us, the pruning begins early in life; others may remain relatively intact until the later decades of life. By no means is all loss pruning, but pruning can certainly look like loss. It can also look like relational fracture or like failure, weakness, or sickness, because it involves paring back in some capacity. God can use it all. If we allow the shears to do their work, the purpose is always the same: growth.

In the pruning of botanical grapevines, however, the process tends to be marked by a certain uniformity. The vines are pruned back each year in the colder months. They go from bush-like plants with multiple appendages to slender canes.

Let me try to paint the picture for you. Keith and I have shared a long affinity for fat Christmas trees. It happened at the start of our marriage when, mind you, Keith was a plumber's helper and such holiday spending was the ultimate in foolhardiness. I blame his family. Mine didn't have a dime at any month's end, so there was little to spare for such luxuries. Keith's family owned a plumbing company, and because people are partial to flushing, the Moores could afford a flocked tree.

I also blame Keith's family for how early we acquire our corpulent tree. When I was growing up in Arkansas, Daddy and Papaw went to the woods, cut down a pine small enough to carry, and hauled it home fresh—and rarely before mid-December. When I became a Houstonian, I discovered people here think Christmas trees appear magically in concrete lots, precut. And since they only get deader, if you want a single needle to survive the drive home, you must make your purchase in mid-November. This is, of course, all foolishness, but I, too, have become a fool.

By December 26, it's all I can do not to command someone in the name of Jesus to get that tree out of my house before I set a match to it, along with every ornament on it. Come New Year's Eve, I don't care when Baby's First Christmas was. Get that tree out.

This is the point at which Keith and I do our best work. We spread out the heavy plastic that's already pre-folded under the tree, fetch two sets of garden shears, cut all the branches nearly to nubs, and let them fall onto the plastic while we look smug. We then pick up what's left of the tree, which now weighs the equivalent of a box of toothpicks, and take it where all good Christmas trees go when they retire: to the curb.

Picture the naked tree trunk on the curb, and you'll have a vague idea of a vine's appearance after a good, thorough pruning. The difference is that the vine is still in the ground and, despite its appearance, a long shot from dead.

Longevity doesn't do much for precut Christmas trees, but age is actually a bonus when it comes to faith. We weathered ones have learned by now how seasons often go and how what sometimes appears to be a fierce killing ends up being a peculiar healing. God has pared us back over and over, and He has made us fruitful again—not always in the same ways, but always in some way. We've learned that barrenness, spiritually speaking, is optional. It's the fruit of uncooperativeness.

From my observations and experience, younger servants are at higher risk of having the shears nick their hearts. The early days of faith tend to require extra measures of pruning to prepare the branch to be most productive. Likewise, experienced gardeners literally nip the blooms of brand-new vines in the bud.

> Any flower clusters that show during these first two
> years should be taken off with clippers or a thumbnail.
> These are the years when proper training is much more
> important than whatever small fruit yield the vine will
> bear. Since fruit yield and vegetative growth compete for
> the vine's resources, allowing fruit to develop will slow
> down the training and you'll get less fruit in the long run.[2]

God doesn't prune everyone by the same hard, fast rule, but every fruitful branch, without exception, will experience cutbacks. Jesus declared this in John 15:2: "He prunes the branches that do bear fruit so they will produce even more" (NLT).

Here's how the pattern frequently goes. The young life awakened in Christ is fresh faced and full of promise. Eyes are full of vision. Heart is full of passion. Ears are full of direction. The young man knows exactly where he's headed. The young woman knows precisely what she's called to be. They each set out on their path and, just about the time they really start to bloom, the clipping ensues. Life gets hard. Affirmation decreases. Passion wanes.

Inspiration dries up. Material doesn't materialize. Clarity turns to cloudiness.

Phase 1 is normally annoyance with God. *You led me here, then left me here. You told me to go, then didn't come through.* Don't be surprised if you experience an ironic sense of lostness just when you thought you'd found what you were looking for. This can be its own form of pruning. It reminds us that what we really want is God. Neither arrival nor achievement can keep us satisfied. Only abiding can.

God never calls us to something only to abandon us once we've arrived. He's at work whether or not we see a whit of evidence.

Phase 2 is self-doubt. *God didn't mislead me; I misled myself. I made it up and called it God.* With this phase usually comes embarrassment, since after all, you told people you'd been called.

The truth is, you were indeed called, and your calling is irrevocable. This setback is for the sake of your calling, not in spite of it. Difficulty is paramount to producing. Without it, you won't be able to faithfully steward your gifting. Without it, your output may exceed your input and prove you to be all skin and no pulp.

Phase 3 is the valley of decision. This is a critical season, because here you will either withdraw to a less vulnerable proximity or cling closer to Jesus despite the appearance of promises aborted. Will you hang around for the training? This becomes the million-dollar question.

At times God is too close for us to see. We lose sight of how He's working until months or years later, when we're able to step back and gain a broader perspective.

I frequently think about Moses pleading with God to show him His glory. God knew Moses couldn't handle what he was requesting, so He told him He'd hide him in the crevice of a rock and cover him with His hand while His glory passed by.

SOMETIMES OUR *growing* COMES IN *shrinking.*

Then I will take away my hand, and you shall see my back,
but my face shall not be seen.

EXODUS 33:23

At times we're in the dark because God is revealing some aspect of His glory that's more than we can stare straight in the face. The beauty in the darkness is that God is close enough to cover us with His hand. Often at the end of a tremendously intense season, He'll grace us with a glimpse of His back. He gives us just enough evidence of His presence for us to realize He was there all along—not as a spectator or even just as a protector, but as Lord over all.

It may be fair to say that God is never closer to us than He is during the pruning process. He can't avoid holding a branch when He's pinching off blooms with His thumbnail. With God as Gardener, pruning is always a hands-on endeavor. He can't let us go when He's cutting us back. His tending is never impersonal. Never mechanical. Never by the long arm of the law.

What most of us didn't expect when we took up with Him was that His presence would sometimes cause pain. We expected His presence to relieve pain and, to our great relief, it usually does. But who would Isaiah have turned out to be without "Woe is me, for I am undone!" (Isaiah 6:5, NKJV)? Or what about David, without the repentant cry "Let the bones that you have broken rejoice" (Psalm 51:8)? Or Job, without "Even if he kills me, I will hope in him" (Job 13:15, CSB)? These slayings were their makings.

They may be ours too. God cuts back a fruitful vine only to increase its fruitfulness. That's why growing can look a lot like shrinking.

+ + +

Several years ago, I was pretty sure I'd dashed most of my ministry to pieces. Even more concerning was the foreign feeling that I was oddly okay with it. *You're depressed,* I told myself. *That's all.* I was, but that wasn't all. I was resigned. *So be it,* I thought.

Fueled by personal conviction, I'd become increasingly outspoken in ways that were at odds with a vocal population of the only Christian world I'd ever known by heart. Over the course of four decades, I've had the pleasure of serving from one extreme of the denominational spectrum to the other and most everything between, but evangelicalism is my native soil. Lifelong relationships have seeded, rooted, and grown in that rich humus.

An evangelical mongrel of sorts, I've never managed to escape controversy, but in the early autumn of 2016, as the first leaves in our woods left their limbs, I made people mad who'd been glad to study Scripture with me for years. I burned some important bridges, unraveled some strong ties, and in the words of the psalmist, tangled with "foes, who were too strong for me" (Psalm 18:17, NIV). The punishment was swift and unrelenting, and the tears, profuse.

The absence of regret makes no guarantee of the absence of pain.

As the weeks set in, so did the realities. Event attendance dropped. Orders dropped. Revenue dropped. Ministry morale dropped. Up to this point, many of my close ministry companions and I had been inseparable. United. Now we were fractured and scattered and uncertain of the future.

Believing our ministry was making a beeline back to small, I started thinking small. These were not despairing thoughts. After all, there are beauties in the miniature that get lost in the masses. I'd long desired to open the doors of our ministry weekly over the noon hour for anyone to stop by for prayer, but my pitch had been voted down over security concerns. Now I determined to overturn it. I announced our start date in less than a month, along with some no-hype worship gatherings, where I'd bring a brief word.

No handouts.

No snacks.

No coffee bar.

No bling.

We'd tell people where to find the water fountain and the restroom. We'd show up that night in whatever we wore to work that morning. We'd shun phones and refuse to record anything. We'd meet in a medium-sized sanctuary and make no attempt to drum up a crowd. We'd keep the worship focus clear and the message uncomplicated.

So these things began, and they brought us back to life.

To unity.

To simplicity.

To joys sufficient to heckle hell.

Every Tuesday, come noon, we put an old-school sign on the curb that said "Need prayer?" And lo and behold, people do. Every week women pull into the parking lot, sometimes eight of them, sometimes eighteen. We're face-to-face again, skin to skin. No barriers. No go-betweens.

They have come with requests ranging from "It's my birthday, and I want prayer for a better year" to "I'm dying of stage 4 kidney cancer." We listen intently to what each person is saying. We hold them in our arms and let them cry, if that's what it takes for them to voice their request. But most of all, we pray, one-on-one or two-on-one, and with enough faith to expect them to return some Tuesday and tell us how God outlandishly answered.

What we didn't expect was for the small things to infuse the big things and for the local ministry to nourish the larger ministry. The downward slide curbed, and though some women kept their word and didn't darken our event doors again, others we'd never seen walked quizzically through them. The old has been made strangely new.

Mind you, God was under no obligation to bring such growth out of the pruning, and furthermore, all the regrowth could wither tomorrow. Remember, the Vinedresser is after quality. God is on to us when our motivation for being cooperative in a cutback is to get back to bigness. His idea of increased fruitfulness may never be humanly measurable. It may be a matter of taste, in the subtle notes of a cluster of grapes that never outgrows a woman's fist.

For the fourteen of us at Living Proof, what has come with thinking small is knowing we can make it. The Lord is our support, as the psalmist said (Psalm 18:18). Not numbers. Not revenue. Not public knownness. Maybe we'll make it for years as a team, or maybe not. If not, we'll make it as individuals, with the Lord's help. Maybe we'll get a paycheck once a month, but if not, we'll volunteer at our churches and find other jobs. All a servant requires is someone to serve.

As long as you can meet somebody's need, you still have purpose. It doesn't take much to matter. It just takes meaning.

Your growing comes in shrinking.

CHAPTER 11

trellis

After I finished speaking at a conference a number of years ago, a woman came up to me, holding her daughter by the hand. The woman looked at me meaningfully and said, "Beth, if you could take a minute, I'd like to introduce you to my daughter."

I love a girl of any age, but I am particularly taken with preadolescents. Something about their being on the very precipice of womanhood makes me want to spend hours with them, shopping or perhaps eating at their favorite place—anywhere I might somehow get the message across, whether through words or actions, that being a woman of God is such a wonderful thing.

I want them to know that Jesus clothes females with strength and dignity. I want them to know that the way the world sometimes treats us is not reflective of Him, nor is it okay with Him.

I leaned forward to speak to this girl, but before I could utter a word, the mom added, "She has a background like yours."

A knife went through my heart, because I understood immediately what she was telling me: this precious girl had experienced some kind of abuse in her young life.

The daughter looked at me and nodded timidly.

With haste, I swallowed the lump in my throat. As much as I wanted to weep over her, to grieve over this broken world in general and this beloved child in particular, I knew that wasn't what she needed from me.

She never took her eyes off mine, undoubtedly searching my face for how she should feel about herself. It was one of those moments when you know you'd better choose your words with utmost care. She needed to know that she mattered. That her pain mattered. That there was hope for her. That she wasn't just meant to survive but to thrive.

So I cupped her face in my hands. "Oh, my goodness," I said. "I am so sorry. But do you know what that means?"

She shook her head.

"That means you get to learn how to be strong in Jesus in a way lots of other people won't. You get to learn who you are in Him and how precious you are to Him, because people like you and me must, in order to have healthy, happy hearts. We get to know Jesus the way some people never bother knowing Him. Somebody very wrong made us feel really small, but now we get to learn how to stand really, really tall."

My words weren't enough, of course.

The arena was crowded and noisy, and we were unable to talk freely. But the girl's wise mother assured me she was surrounded with love, community, and solid counseling.

God doesn't promise that we'll avoid pain because we follow Him. He doesn't promise that we'll escape trauma or abuse or divorce or illness or pain or death. But He does promise a way up. A way through. Or a way out.

If we offer what we've experienced to Him, in all its horror and ugliness, and receive His offer to redeem all that occurred, He will bring fruit from it. This has been the single most healing aspect of my recovery from childhood victimization. This is my prayer for that precious little girl. And my prayer for you, too, if you've experienced something similar.

✝ ✝ ✝

The vinedresser establishes a training system for his vine, or he is no vinedresser at all. This is where the trellis enters the picture. When the trunk of a vine reaches around twelve inches tall, the vinedresser ties it to some form of stake. If he fails to do so, all hopes of a quality harvest are vanquished. With every three or four inches of growth comes another tie. The vinedresser follows suit with the vine's horizontal shoots, tying them securely and strategically onto trellis wires.

Stroll through the rows of any functioning vineyard, and you'll notice that the posture of a grapevine is a direct reflection of the apparatus it's attached to. Simply put, the way it's trained is the way it will grow. The apparatus may be anything from a single grape stake to an elaborate archway trellis, but whatever form it takes, the growing vine needs adequate support. The branches cannot carry the weight of immense fruitfulness on their own.

Besides providing the muscle to keep the vine from drooping, the trellis also offers the vinedresser the structure to spread out the grape canopy and keep it untangled as it grows. Without it, parts of the plant would be bullied into the shadows by more aggressive branches. These weaker branches would then be starved of the sunlight and circulation they need to thrive.

If the vinedresser doesn't take over, the branches will. And if the branches take over, the vine's productivity suffers and the delectable taste of the fruit goes untapped.

Wood and ties. These are essential to a growing vine.

Wood and nails. These were essential to the true Vine.

"I am the true vine, and my Father is the vinedresser," Jesus said (John 15:1). Less than twenty-four hours after voicing these words, the Vinedresser would nail the true Vine to wood. This was all part of the eternal plan.

> *It was the will of the LORD to crush him;*
> *he has put him to grief;*
> *when his soul makes an offering for guilt,*
> *he shall see his offspring; he shall prolong his days;*
> *the will of the LORD shall prosper in his hand.*
>
> ISAIAH 53:10

Salvation was nailed down, once and for all, to that blood-stained wood. No further sacrifice would be required for the remission of sins.

> *Out of the anguish of his soul he shall see and be satisfied;*
> *by his knowledge shall the righteous one, my servant,*
> *make many to be accounted righteous,*
> *and he shall bear their iniquities.*
>
> ISAIAH 53:11

The Cross of Christ is our stake in the ground. It is immovable. It is nonnegotiable. Let others be tied to whatever they please, but we are tied to the Cross. There is no playing it down. There is no dressing it up. There is no gospel without it. No reconciliation with God. No Easter morning resurrection sermon. Should this earth still exist in the year 4000, either the church will still be tied to the Cross or it will be the church of the lost.

Satan is a lot of things, but he's not particularly creative. He tends to stick with what works, and one approach that has paid off for him from the start is our low tolerance for feeling stupid. Rewind to Eden's lush gardens and a clever, conniving serpent. "How could you believe that? What kind of idiot are you?" In a world system under his invasive influence, we have to make peace with looking like fools at times, or the war within our souls will demoralize us.

> *The message of the cross is foolishness to those who are perishing, but to us who are being saved it is the power of God. For it is written:*
>
> *I will destroy the wisdom of the wise;*
> *the intelligence of the intelligent I will frustrate.*
> 1 CORINTHIANS 1:18-19, NIV

The Cross is our stake in the ground. But like the trellis, it is also our training system. There seems to be no limit on what we are willing to spend—in both time and money—on leadership training, job training, parental training, athletic training, potty training, and dog training, but "come and die" training is a harder sell. Yet it remains our only means of finding true life—not just after we shed these temporal bodies, but right here, right now. On this very earth, in this very era, on the very block where we live.

The way of the Cross teaches sacrificial love to otherwise

THE

cross of Christ

IS OUR STAKE IN

THE GROUND.

self-seeking, self-absorbed, self-exalting creatures who can never seem to get enough of themselves to satisfy themselves. Our culture's tireless training in narcissism has not made us happy; it has made us miserable. We're so full of ourselves that we're vomiting ourselves all over our public platforms. We have not broken our mirrors, but our mirrors have broken us, the way Narcissus's obsession with his own reflection ultimately broke him. The way of the Cross is painful, to be sure, but it is also a peculiar relief. Over the long haul, the weight of an unchecked human ego becomes a heavier load to bear than a cross.

To mortals who by nature desire to be sophisticated, clever, and esteemed, God offered a Savior who was "despised and rejected by men" (Isaiah 53:3). To a human race insatiably attracted to attractiveness, God offered a Savior with "no form or majesty that we should look at him, and no beauty that we should desire him" (Isaiah 53:2). We keep looking for a beautiful way to a beautiful life, when as God would have it, the only way to find it is through an unbeautiful cross.

Far be it from me to boast except in the cross of our Lord
Jesus Christ, by which the world has been crucified to me,
and I to the world.
GALATIANS 6:14

God knew it would take a cross to crucify us to the world. The death of His Son by countless other means would bear less stigma, less ridicule, less mess. God chose a means by which we could not have our pride and our salvation too. The message of the Cross preached with pride is equally absurd. We may still attempt it, but it's as ill fitting as King Saul's armor on a shepherd boy with a slingshot.

The training system of the Cross ties the branches of the true Vine to humility. The prouder we are, the further we move away from it.

✝　✝　✝

Without a trellis, the vine would fold in on itself, remaining stuck at ground level. Without a trellis, the branches would never reach their heads up to the sun. And so the trellis of the Cross trains us in the way of forgiveness (Luke 23:33-35). It lifts our heads from the dirt and sludge and raises our faces to the Son—the same Son who prayed from the Cross, "Father, forgive them, for they know not what they do" while strangers gawked at Him, rulers scoffed at Him, and soldiers cast lots for His clothing. An unforgiving Christian is the embodiment of an oxymoron. God help me, I've been one. I suppose we all have. Life hands us plenty of opportunities to practice the dichotomy.

Not every victim of sexual abuse or assault gets an apology from the perpetrator. I did, and in case you're wondering, it wasn't enough. It was begrudging and minimizing and brief and final. Think of it under the "There, I said it" category. "Now let it go."

I forgave—but not because the man wanted me to. I forgave because it's the way of the Cross. I forgave because I realized this man had no idea what he'd done, no idea what his unspeakably selfish actions had cost me or anyone else who may have fallen victim to him. No sooner had the thought gone through my mind, *He has no clue,* than the words from the Cross ran right behind them: "Father, forgive them, for they know not what they do" (Luke 23:34).

I didn't forgive right then. I didn't forgive in any single moment that I recall. I wish I could say I did. I forgave over time. I forgave through teaching, through developing a different mind-set, through praying, through agreeing with Jesus about what to do when I'm wronged.

I've become increasingly convinced that those we need to forgive most often grasp the least how much they've hurt us. If they understood and took responsibility, it wouldn't have taken the Cross to forgive them. It could have just happened over coffee.

The way of the Cross is forgiveness—raw and bloody and gasping for air. It seldom follows earnest shouts of "I'm sorry!" More likely, it's surrounded by the sounds of "Crucify him!"

Father, I forgive them in Christ's name, for they don't get what they did.

These are the kinds of words that resound all the way to the bottom of the darkest abyss. The very things that tie us to the Cross set us free from death and hell.

Sometimes as we train for forgiveness, the greater war is to accept forgiveness ourselves. I could list multiple words off the top of my head to describe the effects of childhood molestation on my life, but I have little to no vocabulary to describe the effects of my own sins. Even with the most tormenting offenses decades behind me, I still plunge my blistered face into Colossians 2:13-15 like a desert wanderer dying of thirst, having belly-crawled miles to a spring.

You, who were dead in your trespasses and the uncircumcision of your flesh, God made alive together with him, having forgiven us all our trespasses, by canceling the record of debt that stood against us with its legal demands. This he set aside, nailing it to the cross. He disarmed the rulers and authorities and put them to open shame, by triumphing over them in him.

COLOSSIANS 2:13-15

Did you catch the banner-waving, demon-defying victory of those words? *Forgiven us all our trespasses . . . canceling the record of debt . . . nailing it to the cross.* If we want to climb the trellis of forgiveness, we have to embrace the truth of these words.

One way the enemy of our souls deflects the shame he experienced at the Cross is to keep us too heaped in our own shame to notice his. The tragedy is that we play right along, as if he were more believable than Jesus.

I recall praying with a woman who approached me at an event, disheveled and overwrought. "I haven't had a shower in weeks," she blurted out, inching toward the edge of hysteria. "I don't know what's wrong with me." She choked out the words, blotting eyes that were flowing like brooks.

My heart bled with compassion as it became clear that she was so convinced of her own filth that she wouldn't let herself bathe. God only knows how many times she'd confessed her sins, but she couldn't accept His forgiveness.

I knew the feeling. I knew what it's like to think that God's grace is poured out in endless waves, drenching everyone else but me. Self-loathing is such a convincing deception. It has an uncanny knack for persuading us to identify ourselves as the exception to every grace.

Words from the inspired pen of a beloved disciple beg to differ:

If we confess our sins, he is faithful and just to forgive us our sins and to cleanse us from all unrighteousness.
1 JOHN 1:9

Cleansed. Purified. Made clean.

We talked that day, this woman and I, about the power of the Cross. We talked about believing the Word of God over the voice of our old self-destructive natures. We talked about the One who "has delivered us from the domain of darkness and transferred us to the kingdom of his beloved Son, in whom we have redemption, the forgiveness of sins" (Colossians 1:13-14). We talked about how the gift of God's grace through Christ Jesus is inconceivably greater than any trespass we could commit (Romans 5:15).

Then we prayed together. I hugged her tightly and said goodbye, and she told me later that she'd gone home to a nice, long shower. I'm not naive enough to think that was the end of her struggle. But I do think it was a beginning. A powerful, brave beginning. And there is no end to any bondage on earth without one.

I didn't recommend to this woman that she promise never to return to her sin and *then* go shower. I've lived too long and studied too hard to miss the fact that behavior is inextricably rooted in belief. As long as she was convinced she was filthy, she would have lacked the wherewithal to last through the next lonely weekend. She didn't need to make promises to God in order to be free. She needed to believe the promises God had made to her.

Forgive, believer, because you've been forgiven. Forgive yourself. Forgive them. Forgive, because those who have devastated you are oblivious to the depths of what they've done. Forgive, because this is the way of the Cross. Forgive, because this is the rolling landscape that causes a world-weary wanderer to stop and gaze at a vineyard, curiosity piqued, arrested by the rare beauty of it all. Come and behold "vines stretched on their trellises, their arms wide open in welcome, or, in a different light, resembling rows of the crucified."[1]

This is our training. Our trellis. When the branch abides in the Vine, forgiveness is wholly unobstructed. It flows freely, both vertically and horizontally.

Welcome, one and all, to the way of the Cross.

PART 4

The Fruit

Unless a grain of wheat falls
into the earth and dies, it remains alone;
but if it dies, it bears much fruit.

JOHN 12:24

CHAPTER 12

soil

I have been thinking a lot about soil lately, because we put our dearly loved bird dog's lifeless body in the ground not long ago.

Until just a few generations ago, death was something that was handled in a very personal way. People prepared and dressed the bodies of their deceased family members and then displayed them in their own homes for the visitation. When it was time for the burial, they helped dig their loved ones' graves.

Any other way would have been completely foreign to my maternal grandparents, who lived in a rural community in Arkansas. On three separate occasions, they lost three deeply cherished children, one at just under six weeks old and the others around the age of two.

We have a picture of one of the two-year-olds, dressed carefully and tucked safely in the small pine box, all cradle-like. And while most people today would find such a picture morbid or disturbing, our family holds it sacred.

I'm told that just after Anthony died, my grandmother sobbed to my grandfather that they didn't have a single picture of him to remember him by. He did what any good husband would do: he hunted down the closest man with a camera. The picture was among her dearest possessions until the day she died at the age of eighty-seven.

Today, we tend to hold death—and dirt itself, for that matter—at arm's length. We outsource death and burial to funeral parlors and crematories, almost as if we think we can ward it off by not letting it come too close. By no means am I suggesting that our ways of dealing with death are wrong (I'm not planning to have a casket in my house either). But our ways of mourning have moved a long way in a few short generations.

Whether we acknowledge it or not, death, by God's design, is part of the cycle that eventually brings new life. It's the very decaying elements in the soil that make it rich and fertile for growth. As Scripture says, "For you are dust, and to dust you shall return" (Genesis 3:19).

+ + +

Geli (pronounced "jelly") was a nine-and-a-half-year-old German shorthaired pointer that never outgrew her naughtiness. We acquired her along with a border collie I named Queen Esther within a few weeks, when they were each two months old. It seemed like a good idea at the time. Since then, we've sworn and declared never to get two puppies again, because as darling as they were, the damage they did to our home and yard was akin to demonic.

Geli and Esther were three years old when we forsook a city fence for the freedom of the woods, and not one day was wasted on them. Collars were optional, and dog leashes were long forgotten in utility room drawers. The two would whine obnoxiously every morning until I'd finally finish my devotions, put on my snake boots, and throw the door wide open. Geli would take off like a shot on her long, lithe legs, while my short-legged Queen ran huffing and puffing in her wake. They romped through those woods every day for six years, dragging their bellies through every mud hole, chasing critters, and rolling enthusiastically in every smidge of carrion.

But freedom is never free, and no one paid more dearly for liberty than Geli. She sustained four separate snake bites and was no worse for the wear, with the exception of our debit card, since getting bitten during regular vet hours was apparently out of the question. Losing an eyeball to a raccoon in a skirmish was considerably harder to overcome, but she managed valiantly. In the last year of her life, she all but lost the use of her back right leg to arthritis, but the way she saw it through her one eye, why slow down with three perfectly good legs?

In an ideal world, wise owners with an increasingly infirmed dog would limit their pet to the indoors and a fenced backyard. The problem was that Geli would rather have choked to death on a possum carcass than be permanently confined. So at least once every day, that baby got to hit the trail and run like a greyhound. It was what she lived for.

And ultimately what she died for.

Keith was out of town one morning in the bowels of West Texas but was scheduled to be home by early evening. Before work that morning, Melissa and her Weimaraner and my two dogs and I went for a hike through the woods. Due to Geli's disabilities, I often gave her a short head start so the other two dogs wouldn't bump into her. But by the time we finished our walk, we hadn't met up with her yet.

"That danged dog," I complained. "She's going to make me late for work."

I spent the next several hours walking all over those woods. I later looked at my steps, as calculated on my phone, and during that time, I put in well over six miles amid those pines, oaks, and sycamores. I also bloodied up my hand tearing through thick, stubborn vines. But I heard nothing. Not one peep.

About one o'clock in the afternoon, my mind played host to a horrifying thought. That morning, several minutes into our walk, Melissa and I had heard horrendous, hair-raising sounds coming from behind us. A cacophony of howls was followed by the yelps of a single dog that were so loud and long we stopped in our tracks, grabbing each other by the arm. I knew something awful had happened somewhere beyond our property. I felt such pity for whatever soul owned and loved that suffering dog.

I usually know when I'm feeling sorry for myself but not this time. It never once occurred to Melissa or me that those sounds were coming from Geli. We couldn't have imagined that she would have gotten so far so fast, and after all, everybody who lives in the country has dogs. But by 4:30 that afternoon, I was almost physically ill. I knew in my gut that it had been her. Still, I hiked and called, but only at a whisper, because by now, all I could do was sob.

Keith said he'd be home by 5:15 p.m., but he wasn't. When I called him, he answered the phone happily and expectantly. "You found my dog?"

"No. Where are you?"

"I'm fifteen minutes out."

"Keith, don't even come in the house. Meet me at the golf cart. We'll only have minutes before it gets dark."

At 5:30 he pulled into the driveway, and we both hopped into an old golf cart capable of getting to places in the woods our cars couldn't reach. I told him what I'd heard.

"Lizabeth," he calls me. "I want you to direct me as close to the place where you heard that sound as you possibly can. I trust your hearing. Now take me there."

I turned him to the right, over our small bridge and up through a field, and to the right again, down a thin path. Then I said, "Stop." I pointed to vines so thick they looked like a snaky black wall against the twilight. "I heard the yelping coming from over there."

Keith tore through the vines as the thorns tore the flesh of his forearms. When he got to the other side, I saw a flash of white. "Was that her?"

"Nope," he yelled back. "A deer." A whitetail.

He returned several minutes later. I'll spare you the next few minutes except to say that, as the darkness fell, those woods heard a woman cry as loud as a dog had yelped at the break of day.

As best as we could piece together, Geli had playfully chased a half dozen deer through the woods and onto that property. Then she ran straight into what we assumed was a pack of coyotes.

Keith spotted Geli's paws first. The rest of her lifeless body was covered by leaves. Even though he knew she was dead, he whispered, "Thank You, God. Thank You, God," with every step he took toward her.

Now this is not a very religious man. I'd have put my money on him cussing a blue streak. But the way he saw it, at least we wouldn't have to wonder where she was or imagine her sweet little self, with her beautiful white coat and big brown spots, out there in the elements all night long. We had the smallest window of time to find her, and God made sure we did.

Angelina "Geli" Moore, our nine-year-old bird dog with one eye and three legs, would be safe and sound in our garage, wrapped in her soft bedspread for the night. And the next day we'd put her in the ground.

+ + +

Our son-in-law Curtis came early to help Keith dig a deep grave in a clearing under what we call the Bent Pine. It's our favorite tree on the property, deeply rooted and gnarly, with a thick trunk. It looms four stories tall, with bright green needles twice as long as your fingers, even in the dead of winter. It would be a prize-winning pine, except that its slender neck and green-needled head bend severely to the left. The Bent Pine has been through a lot, we figure, and while it has never quite overcome the effects of the elements that arced it, it also refused to not grow and flourish. Keith and I built the house close to it because it reminds us of ourselves—still a bit maimed, but for the most part hearty and unashamed.

I wish I could get by without telling you this part of the story, but it won't be nearly as honest or eccentric without it. Keith and Curtis dug the grave next to those of Geli and Queen Esther's predecessors. Yes, we had their bones exhumed and transferred them to our property in the country. So what? We weren't going to leave them with strangers. If you need a supporting verse, I present to you Joseph, the favored son of Jacob, whose bones were packed up like so much baggage and carried shamelessly to the Promised Land when the Hebrew people departed Egypt. I shall neither exegete nor supply anything further.

The rest of the family arrived early that afternoon for the informal graveside service. Keith looked seven feet tall to me that day, his shoulders so broad and his lined face brown and handsome. This was his bird dog, his constant shadow, and he'd feel her absence more than any of us, yet he guided us through the burial with the gentleness and wisdom of a pastor. I can't say I've ever seen exactly that in him before.

He smiled lovingly and reassuringly at all of us, then knelt down beside Geli's body. He'd wrapped it carefully in one of the blankets she slept on every night of her life, safe and sound inside our home, not far from us. Like a shepherd, the man said to all his lambs, "We're gathered here to entrust our sweet Geli's body to the earth and to be thankful for her and to share our favorite stories about her."

And so we told our stories. Most of them had something to do with how naughty she was, but aren't most of the best dogs also the worst? We talked about how unstoppable she was. Determined. Adventurous. Hilarious. Then Keith and I lowered her into the deep hole and gently set her down. He invited whoever wanted to participate to throw in a couple of handfuls of earth, and then he put his hands on his hips, looked at me, and said, "I think that's all I can do today."

"Baby," I replied, "I've got this from here."

The men retreated to the house with our two-year-old grand-daughter, Willa, who was superbly oblivious to the whole ordeal.

"It's the steel magnolias," Amanda quipped, an endearment from the iconic late eighties movie she uses for our foursome: her plucky nine-year-old daughter, Annabeth; her sister, Melissa; her mother; and her. We offered colorful verbal affirmations, picked up the shovels, and filled in every teaspoon of space with soil. Annabeth and I then packed it down carefully as if we were walking on a grave in ballet slippers. Never mind that Melissa placed white roses tied with a burlap ribbon at the head of it while Amanda and Annabeth scattered multicolored rose petals around the edges. Such notions might be pearls before swine. Let each do what one must to mourn.

There were no dry eyes that day, but no one mourned like Queen Esther, who sat close by, in quiet observance, wearing her usual black with a white fur bib. When we finished our task, we girls sat across from the grave together, Annabeth and I flanking the Queen, hugging her, kissing her head, and telling her that she'd make it because we'd see to it. Lest we be confused enough to assume we were feeling the same thing as she, the collie promptly stepped away from us and sat down squarely on Geli's grave, alone, and looked away from us.

Let the reader who thinks nine years was plenty long to have a good dog admit to their shame that they have neither had a good dog nor loved one.

We've always placed the bodies of our pets in the ground when they were finished with them. The practice is not one of conviction as much as preference, and I should admit to the privilege of having access to a place. It's difficult to plant a fifty-pound daisy of a bird dog in a garden bath—and chancy, if you don't plan on staying awhile.

Somehow we've always had a yard when the occasion arose, and despite the innumerable topics Keith and I see differently on, we've managed to feel the exact same way about this one: we entrust our dogs' bodies to the ground, because we respect the ground. We'd actually prefer the same protocol for our own bodies when we're finished with them. Just dig a deep hole at the bottom of a hill, hurl us on a four-wheeler, drop us off sans casket, give us a good shove, and then let us roll down yonder. Please do, however, clothe us in biodegradable frocks—preferably pantaloons rather than saintly robes, as robes have a way of hiking up in a fast roll. We see no need to make our exits excessively memorable for those dear enough to gather at our final resting place.

I realize all of this is a pipe dream. Our daughters are of tender conscience, and we suspect they will not share our agrarian enthusiasm. Nevertheless, God originated the idea Himself: "By the sweat of your face you shall eat bread, till you return to the ground, for out of it you were taken; for you are dust, and to dust you shall return" (Genesis 3:19).

Psalm 104 speaks poignantly of God's watchful care over the animals of the fields and depicts Him feeding them from His own open hand. When the time comes, He takes "away their breath, they die and return to their dust" (verse 29).

I know the thought seems morbid to most, but to Keith and me, something about it simply seems right. Those romping canines of ours, now stilled, are sown right into our land, nourishing the deep broad roots of one fine Bent Pine.

✦ ✦ ✦

The hill Isaiah spoke of could have been the most spectacular spot on earth, with perfect aspect and magnificent aesthetics. It could have been hemmed in by a wall of gleaming limestone and guarded from a grand limestone tower, with no expense spared. But if its soil hadn't been fertile, all would have been futile.

My beloved had a vineyard on a very fertile hill.

Merriam-Webster's definition of the word *fertile* is as far as we'd have to look for proof of a connection between fertile ground and fruit bearing. The first definition sounds like it could be describing the hillsides of Tuscany: "producing or bearing fruit in great quantities; productive."

The other definitions include similar words, such as *producing,* *bearing, sustaining,* and *reproducing.* Each term is rooted like a deep vine in the meaning of the word *fertile.*

The English Standard Version doesn't stop at saying the hill upon which God planted His vineyard was fertile. It says the hill was *very* fertile. So what constitutes very fertile soil? My research took me further underground than I meant to go. With your patience, I'll take you there with me, and if you're willing to make it through some technicalities, I believe it will pay off.

As journalist and author Andrew Jefford puts it, "There is no branch of agriculture in which soils are more rhapsodized and venerated than in viticulture."[1] Viticulturists may have unknowingly inherited a certain rhapsody of the soil simply by being image bearers of the Creator. After all, soil is the dark and lovely porous skin of this astronomical body on which we spin. So let the rhapsody begin.

Let's pretend you've been inspired to plant a few common-variety grapevines on a plot of land nearby. Maybe your climate isn't perfect, but you still want to give it a shot, because frankly, your home is where it is and your climate is all you've got. You've chosen a sunny spot with enough aspect to drain well so as not to drown the tender plant. You've looked into the varieties of grapes that tend to be most forgiving to well-meaning neophytes. You've researched whether other vinedressers in your region have had at least moderate success. You're on the verge of placing your vine order. What do you do next?

You take your shovel and dig a hole several feet deep, gather up a sample of the soil into a clean container, and either send it to a soil-testing lab for analysis (available in most counties) or use a kit to test it yourself. The former method is preferable, not simply because beginner's luck is overrated, but because your soil has a personality profile you might enjoy getting to know. Think of it as an Enneagram test for dirt. All sorts of interesting elements turn up in the soil—positives you want to accentuate and negatives you want to learn how to navigate.

The specifics may vary depending on where you live, but chances are your soil is a loam—a combination of clay, silt, sand, stones, and organic matter. To have the best chance at flourishing, the grapes would prefer a combination of all of the above.[2]

My good friend Fred Billings has been captivated by soil and what makes things grow since he was a teen. It was soil that drove him like an old Ford pickup straight to Texas A&M University, where he majored in agricultural economics, with an emphasis in international trade. That's why I summoned Fred to my office, set up a video camera, and interviewed him for several hours about soil. I don't know many people who could wax on about dirt for so long, but it's his vocation and his passion.

To Keith and me, he is Farmer Fred, and more often, just plain Farmer. He's a brilliant man and an exemplary husband and father, but the best thing about Farmer is that Jesus is the supreme love of his life. Every other passion is viewed through the spectacles of the Spirit. The end game for Farmer is not merely a fascination with soil and what can be organically grown in it. His interest in agriculture ultimately stems from a fascination with the God who created and contrived the whole extraordinary process. His near-lifelong pursuit has produced in him something the world is increasingly dispossessing and begging to rediscover: wonder.

At six foot four, Farmer is an imposing figure who could practically pull a tractor out of a ditch with his bare hands. Yet tears pool in his eyes as he describes the wonders of God waiting to be discovered as we dig into the world of agriculture. Isaiah isn't the only one with a song in his heart when it comes to rhapsodies of the soil. Here's the revelation he shared with me about that unsung hero we track into the house on the bottom of our boots and mop up, with annoyance, off our floors:

> The soil eats, drinks, and breathes, just like we do. What it eats, it also digests. All of this is occurring through a process you can't see, but I can tell you this: the top of the plant never lies.

The analogy left me wide eyed and slack jawed. Christ said the same thing using different vernacular when He told His disciples that they would be able to recognize a tree by its fruit. It would be hard to overstate the role of fruit bearing in a follower's life. That would be like dear Jack pole-vaulting over his enormous beanstalk. Whenever Jesus files something under the category "By this my Father is glorified" (John 15:8), it calls for high billing in our list of priorities.

Remember, Jesus likes watching things grow. He used numerous agricultural metaphors in His teaching, partly because growth is integral to both personal discipleship and to the propagation of the gospel, and also because the world He was speaking to was largely agrarian. With few exceptions, livelihoods in His day were tied to the land or the sea. The art of the parable is to lay the known beside the unknown to make something of the unknown known.

In the parable of the sower, Jesus told a story to a massive crowd about a farmer who went out to sow his seed.

SOME VARIETY
OF DYING

RESURRECTION
LIVING.

*As he sowed, some fell along the path and was trampled
underfoot, and the birds of the air devoured it. And some fell
on the rock, and as it grew up, it withered away, because it
had no moisture. And some fell among thorns, and the thorns
grew up with it and choked it. And some fell into good soil
and grew and yielded a hundredfold." As he said these things,
he called out, "He who has ears to hear, let him hear."*
LUKE 8:5-8

The parable is utter perfection, with multiple layers and players.
Perhaps the disciples feared themselves among those who lacked ears
to hear, because they asked Him what the parable meant. This was a
wise move, since Jesus offered the interpretation without hesitation.

*Now the parable is this: The seed is the word of God. The
ones along the path are those who have heard; then the devil
comes and takes away the word from their hearts, so that
they may not believe and be saved. And the ones on the rock
are those who, when they hear the word, receive it with joy.
But these have no root; they believe for a while, and in time
of testing fall away. And as for what fell among the thorns,
they are those who hear, but as they go on their way they are
choked by the cares and riches and pleasures of life, and their
fruit does not mature. As for that in the good soil, they are
those who, hearing the word, hold it fast in an honest and
good heart, and bear fruit with patience.*
LUKE 8:11-15

This parable echoes Isaiah's song for the Beloved. Both accounts
make it clear that growing things requires soil—and not just any
kind of soil. So what makes soil fertile and therefore good?

The answer may surprise you. Good soil is a curious and compelling combination of life and death. So vital is death to the soil that life cannot exist there without it. The decaying matter from animals and plants is an essential source of nutrients in sustaining life.

Take a teaspoon from your kitchen drawer and dig up one spoonful of healthy soil, and you'll hold in your steady hand multimillions of microorganisms in one of the most impressive combinations of living matter known to humankind. According to Farmer,

There are different kinds of microorganisms that live in the soil, so they have different average lifespans. The maximum is about twelve hours. The minimum is about three minutes. So they live, work, multiply, and die—all of them within twelve hours, and most of them within about twenty minutes.

Not all the organisms in soil are microscopic, as any four-year-old would gladly prove in the palm of his darling, grubby hand, nor are they exempt from this cycle of life and death that makes dirt fertile. According to Robert E. White, "Life in the soil is a struggle." Everything from the tiniest bacteria, invisible to the human eye, to insects and earthworms feed on other organisms, and then they themselves become food for other life forms.[3]

All sorts of things opposed to proper sensibilities become ingredients for fertile soil, including wiggly things, dirty things, and dead things.

Had you never picked up this book, you might have gone to your grave not knowing the identity of the unsung hero of the vineyard's fertile ground: earthworms. I don't know how to say this delicately, but the earthworm's primary contribution to fertile soil comes by way of their hind parts. "Soil . . . becomes more uniformly mixed and deposited in the worm feces." When the feces dry, they "improve soil structure overall."[4]

We tend to think that, if we were God, we'd have come up with different methods. But fortunately for everyone on earth, including us, we're not Him. And from the depths of His inscrutable wisdom, He designed His own methodologies.

If I were in charge, I'd want only life in the soil where I've been planted, not death—and certainly not worm feces. The idea that life alone should give way to life makes perfect sense at first blush. But we who are in Christ know better than that. We know that everlasting life came from Jesus' death. He said Himself, "Truly, truly, I say to you, unless a grain of wheat falls into the earth and dies, it remains alone; but if it dies, it bears much fruit" (John 12:24).

We also know that some variety of dying precedes resurrection living. That's how salvation goes, but it's also how the saved grow. God knows that the most fertile soil for growing anything of value, certainly anything that bears fruit, is a well-blended, purposeful mass of life and death, of germination and decay.

✦   ✦   ✦

In order to adequately appreciate the role of fertile soil, let's take some time to view ourselves within the metaphor. You are a planting of the Lord, and your soil is a blend of elements He is using to grow you in symbiotic cooperation with the absolute necessities of sun and rain. All sorts of conditions are being orchestrated over your head and under your feet to enhance your growth, and much of it is beyond the vision of your naked eye.

The most vital underground element for any plant is called the rhizosphere, "the cylinder of soil surrounding each plant root."[5]

In Farmer's words, it's "where the real life takes place. The rhizosphere is the interface where the root touches the soil. Where that interface connects is where all the life happens."

For the sake of our present metaphor, you, a planting of the Lord, have your own rhizosphere. You are rooted in a cylinder of soil, and for that soil to be good and fertile ground where you can flourish, it must be a mass of all manner of organic matter: bacteria, algae, fungi, yeasts, protozoa, bugs, earthworms, and the like.

Imagine it. If you are planted in really rich soil, that means one little teaspoon holds millions of microbes. It also produces ample evidence of both life and death. In other words, all of it matters. Even unwanted endings. Even crushing losses. Even death itself.

I don't know what your soil looks like at this point in your life, but I'm going to guess that, unless you're among the rarest exceptions, something terrible has happened to you at one point or another. If you have enough years and maturity to get this far in life, your soil already possesses multiple elements that make it fertile—if you're willing to let God use these messy parts to grow you instead of you fighting them off like the most monstrous of foes.

Tossed right alongside the teeming life in your soil, death resides—ready, humble, and willing to enrich and increase all that lives. All sorts of deaths become humus in the ground of the human experience.

Of *your* human experience. Of mine.

This may mean the death of some dreams. The death of some hopes. The death of plans. The death of certain relationships. Perhaps the death of your parents' marriage, or your own marriage. Maybe it means the death of a close friendship. The death of love. The death of romance. Maybe it means the death of an engagement or a deep commitment. The death of an educational opportunity. The death of a career path. The death of an identity. The death of a long-term project that came to nothing. The death of a season of felicity. The sudden death of stability.

Perhaps you've been through the death of a church, whether or not the church even knew it was dead. Maybe you've endured the death of innocence or the death of resolute optimism. Or the death of a parent's memory of you. Or the death of your memories of someone else. And sometimes worst of all, the physical death of someone you loved.

Don't tell me death isn't already in your soil. I won't believe you. And here's the big reveal: it didn't kill you. It didn't kill me, either. I thought it would. I bet you did too. But here we are, you and me, very much alive. Whether we wanted to be or not.

We're plantings of the Lord, in cylinders of soil already plenty fertile. The remaining question—and no small one, at that—is not whether we have what it takes to be extraordinarily fruitful but whether we're willing to expose our tender roots to the odd concoction of life and death that makes us grow.

What use are we here on this earth without a whit of death in our soil? What depth do we have? What fruit? What proof do we have of our faith? What evidence of perseverance? What do we have to say to people in need, in pain, in doubt, in despair? How can we help those who feel nothing but dead if we've known nothing of death ourselves? What glimpse do we have to offer of a Savior whose death gave us life?

So on those days when it seems like God is silent and you have nothing to show for your life besides dung and death, know that even those are not wasted. God is using even the messiest parts and the most painful and seemingly hopeless parts to get your soil ready. You, loved and chosen by God, have much good fruit yet to bear.

CHAPTER 13

roots

When I was twenty-three and Keith was twenty-four, we got a phone call that would forever divide the timeline of the Moore family into two distinct periods: before and after.

We'd just gotten home from church and a quick lunch at a pizza place. I was rocking Amanda to sleep so I could tuck her in for a Sunday afternoon nap. Keith answered the phone, and after uttering a spine-chilling "What did you say?" his knees buckled before my eyes.

Within two minutes, the three of us were in the car, heading furiously to a hospital on the other side of Houston. His sister, a newlywed my age, had suffered a brain aneurysm and wasn't expected to live. We made it in time to spend the rest of the day with her, alongside Keith's parents, two other sisters, and his sister's young husband.

We buried her several days later.

I'd been in the family for only two years, but I clearly remember thinking that life would never be the same. The destruction felt final somehow, like it could never be overcome. Keith's sister was the second child his parents had lost, and they adored her. I was certain it would finish them.

Dark, long days and months followed. I think most of the time when light comes back into our lives, it works more like a dimmer than a switch. There wasn't one particular moment the light switch flipped. A sliver of light would slip in, and we'd huddle close and try to sun our faces before the darkness descended again—and it always did.

Our family's grief, as it is for most people, came in gradations of black to gray. Life never was the same again—it can't be after that kind of loss. But by God's grace, the sun did come out from behind the clouds again, and often enough to warm the blood in our cold bones.

We laughed again. We celebrated special occasions again. We embraced new family members, doted over babies, and slowly returned to the land of the living. We rediscovered how to do simple things like shop for groceries without feeling like our feet were going to come out from under us before we made it to the milk section.

We never forgot. We've never quit talking about her. But our family stayed intact. We've had good years together, and not one have we taken for granted.

✝   ✝   ✝

At one point in Israel's history, God's beloved vine needed reassurance that despite the current heartache, there was reason to hope. They would find their footing again.

Isaiah 37 opens to the soundtrack of Judah's King Hezekiah

ripping his garments in great distress over Assyria's invasion. The Assyrian empire's King Sennacherib had brazenly mocked God as he threatened His people with full-scale disaster. In this context, God sent merciful assurances to Hezekiah through the prophet Isaiah, and then God launched a few threats of His own.

Allow me to paraphrase a few particular highlights of the message God passed to the Assyrian king through Isaiah. Thus saith the Lord:

Who do you think you're talking to? (Isaiah 37:23).
I know where you live (Isaiah 37:28).

God then directed stirring words straight to Hezekiah and the people of Judah:

This shall be the sign for you: this year you shall eat what grows of itself, and in the second year what springs from that. Then in the third year sow and reap, and plant vineyards, and eat their fruit. And the surviving remnant of the house of Judah shall again take root downward and bear fruit upward. For out of Jerusalem shall go a remnant, and out of Mount Zion a band of survivors. The zeal of the LORD of hosts will do this.

ISAIAH 37:30-32

In essence, God's reassurance to His people consisted of this message: *on the other side of this catastrophe, you will once again find normalcy.* The boots of the gargantuan Assyrian army had stomped all over Judah, camping around her fortified cities, shutting in her inhabitants. The Israelites had little to no access to their fields, and what crops the marauders failed to consume, they razed.

From the look of things, no one and nothing would survive, but as God relentlessly reminds His people throughout Scripture, *Take care not to judge from the look of things. I'm at work in ways you cannot see.*

When we're going through a difficult season, wouldn't the best news of all be that life would simply go back to normal someday? When the framework of our daily existence gets completely dismantled and the landscape around us grows increasingly unrecognizable, our strongest longing is seldom prosperity. What we yearn for is normalcy. We don't tend to ask for the moon when we've lost all we've known. We just want some semblance of our old lives back.

The hard truth is, there's no real going back. But once we get up again, there can be a going forward. In His faithfulness, God sees to it what we thought was the end isn't the end after all. And eventually, perhaps not terribly long after, we realize we've transitioned into a new normal.

Take a look at the slice of everyday life God used to represent the remnant's gradual return to normalcy in Isaiah. Even on the heels of the devastation of the Promised Land, God still cared deeply about its terroir, its sense of place. As is often true in the Bible's references to vineyards, the prophetic message Isaiah delivered carries both material and spiritual meaning. Judah would physically plant, grow, and reap again, but these acts were not to be assumed as the natural course of things. They were to be clearly understood as signs that God had performed what He'd promised.

Just finding normal again can be fingerprints of the supernatural.

Unwanted changes occur. Crises happen. Catastrophes invade our days without warning. The enemy comes to steal, kill, and destroy. He wages threats and makes good on some of them. From all appearances, the pleasant field that once surrounded us—increasingly pleasant, in retrospect—has been scorched and razed. However, God makes threats of His own, and He never wastes His breath. Whether or not our physical surroundings ever again resemble what we once knew, if we have an ounce of breath on the other side, we can bear much fruit again.

Maybe right now that promise doesn't mean a lot. You don't want a remnant; you want all the same people back. And truth be told, you'd prefer them at all their former ages and stages. You don't want to grow something new. You want to return to your old life. You want those exact clusters of grapes, not new ones. You want everything to taste exactly like it once did.

I understand. But in time, finding fruitfulness again will make more difference than you can imagine. If we can't have our treasured yesterday back, at least tomorrow can matter. The wonder of fruit bearing is that something meaningful can come from the meanest of seasons. What we endured matters.

+ + +

"And this shall be the sign for you."

The prophecy was to Judah, but the image of an eternal God's faithfulness to His people throughout all generations is breathtaking. In the first year after a catastrophe, we may want to survive on what little there is. The second year, we try to make it on scraps and memories. But maybe, just maybe, in the third year, we put shoulder to shovel and sow again. I should mention here that for many of us, a "year" may not be a dozen months. That time stamp merely offers an illustration of the passage of time. It serves as a flicker of hope to eyes blinded by pain that something—anything—could have meaning again.

There's something I want to clarify here before we get any further: making it matter doesn't mean making it worth it. Embracing the distinction can be no small relief.

One of the biggest obstacles to finding new life, new productiveness, and a new normal is the terror of feeling forced to choose whether what we've been through was worth what we gained. With less costly sacrifices, coming to a "worth it" conclusion tends to be easier. Was losing your job worth keeping your convictions? Was the hard work of reconstructing that relationship worth having the person back in your life? Though you wouldn't want to endure it again, in all likelihood, you'd be able to answer affirmatively, "Yes, it was worth it."

But try these scenarios on for size: Was the nonprofit that was created out of your tragedy worth it? Was the ability to empathize with others worth the people you've lost? Imagine such a question posed to Jerry Sittser, author of *A Grace Disguised: How the Soul Grows through Loss*: "Jerry, have all the people you've helped been worth the catastrophic loss of your wife, daughter, and mother?" How many testimonies would it take? One hundred? One thousand? Ten thousand? Such thoughts are absurd, and such questions, cruel.

Yes, Christ can bring fruit from His followers' incalculable suffering. But on this side of eternity, the point isn't making it worth it. It's about making it matter. *Jesus* is worth it. He's worth trusting. He's worth anticipating. He's worth getting out of bed for when you wish you could go to sleep and never wake up. You may have to believe that by faith until faith becomes sight.

There can be fruit in your life again. That's what I really want you to know. In the words of the prophet Isaiah, "The surviving remnant of the house of Judah shall again take root downward and bear fruit upward" (Isaiah 37:31).

The order is irreversible:

Take root downward.

Bear fruit upward.

Down is the way up with God. There's no bearing fruit upward without first taking root downward. There are no shortcuts. No special dispensations. No exceptions for exceptional people. No special entitlements. Oh, it may seem so for a while, but a shallowly rooted plant won't pass the test of time.

In the parable of the sower, Jesus describes what happens when plants don't take root. People can respond to His words with open arms and ecstatic joy, but if they don't take root, "they believe for a while, and in time of testing fall away" (Luke 8:13).

The shoot can't last without the root.

+ + +

On average, the roots of grapevines are deeper than those of comparable plants. They can plunge to depths of more than twenty feet. If that sounds unimpressive, take a look at the ceiling over your head and estimate its height. If it's a typical nine- or ten-foot ceiling, double it in your mind's eye and then picture roots of a single grapevine going that deep.

In order to bear fruit upward, we take root downward. But how, exactly, do the roots remain anchored in the soil? Essentially, the roots need to collect water and nutrients so the plant can remain secured in the soil. And so it is for us. Even if our soil is good, it won't matter if our roots aren't secure. If we're not firmly anchored, there's little hope that the dormant branch will bud in spring.

Paul describes the essential nutrient our roots need:

According to the riches of his glory he may grant you to be strengthened with power through his Spirit in your inner being, so that Christ may dwell in your hearts through faith—that you, being rooted and grounded in love, may have strength to comprehend with all the saints what is the breadth and length and height and depth, and to know the love of Christ that surpasses knowledge, that you may be filled with all the fullness of God.

EPHESIANS 3:14-19

The trouble with hearing something repeatedly is that our ears grow dull until the most magnificent news hits us with all the magic of a McDonald's drive-thru menu. Whether this passage from Ephesians is something you've known for decades or is a fresh revelation, I believe Jesus can speak to the dullness of our hearing and open our ears (Mark 7:34). I have come to believe that healthy, sustainable growth and immense fruit bearing feed from a single source: knowing we are immeasurably, immutably loved by Christ.

When this truth is more deeply rooted than any other belief we hold, even the fiercest tempest won't be able to rip us from the ground. Our leaves may be frayed and our branches bent, but our roots will hold fast.

But we can't just assume our roots are anchored in the right place. All sorts of competing beliefs vie for that coveted spot. To test what a few contenders might be, I pitched the following questions to individuals in two separate groups—my ministry staff and an audience at a speaking event.

What is your most deeply held belief?
What, beneath all else, are you most convinced is true?

Once we agreed to resist the temptation of offering impressive answers, here's a smattering of responses I received:

> *This world will kill you, so stay on the run. If it catches you,*
>   *you're dead.*
> *Always be ready to jump. There's no room for relaxing. A shoe*
>   *could drop at any time.*
> *God always wants something different from what I want. If*
>   *I really want it, it won't be God's will. My desire jinxes what*
>   *I'll get.*
> *Life is best lived under the radar. Don't be noticeable. Keep*
>   *everything smooth. Calm is the key.*
> *If people don't notice me, I'm not viable. Unseen equals*
>   *unimportant.*
> *I am responsible. I have to keep everything going, or it will all*
>   *fall apart.*
> *I have to be a success to be successful.*
> *I am almost enough. If only I could be more or do just a*
>   *little more.*

I don't ask other people questions I'm not willing to answer. The last answer was mine for more years of my life than I wish to count.

Each of the people participating in this conversation has an active relationship with Christ, and few of them were unaware of their commitment to a false belief. Although they wanted the gospel to be their most closely held belief, these other roots seemed

WE CAN'T HAVE
OUR TREASURED
YESTERDAY BACK,
BUT AT LEAST
TOMORROW
 *can matter.*

too deeply entrenched to unearth. The false beliefs had been in place as long as they could remember.

Other answers seemed spiritual enough to be acceptable.

I love God. That I know deepest of all.

If we dig down far enough, many of us who serve God would discover we're more deeply convinced of our love for Him than of His love for us. When life beats the love right out of us, what happens then?

The Bible is true. That's what I believe most of all.

Yes, it is. Praise God, it is. There's nothing else like it. However, the Bible is not a person who can wrap His everlasting arms around you when you're free-falling into a canyon of despair. Only God Himself can do that.

Let me share just one more faulty conviction.

I believe in love. I believe love saves.

Yes, but whose love? Or is this about love in general? Faith in love for love's sake is a universal winner on social media, but it's pathetically impotent to anchor a person through basic upheaval, to say nothing of an earthquake.

Let's say the belief in love is not general. Let's say the deepest part of your belief system resides in the love of family or, more specifically, a parent, a spouse, a child, a sibling, or a friend.

It's a gift to be so loved. Treasure it. Embrace it. Flourish in it. Reciprocate it. But what happens when a parent grows old? Or a child grows up? Or a friend grows cold? Or a spouse dies?

Only one love cannot let go. Only one love refuses to ebb and flow despite the conditions. There's just one thing "neither death nor life, nor angels nor rulers, nor things present nor things to come, nor powers, nor height nor depth, nor anything else in all creation," will be able to separate us from—"the love of God in Christ Jesus our Lord" (Romans 8:38-39).

Nothing is natural about planting your roots in the soil of the resolute knowledge that you are personally, immeasurably, and immutably loved by God. Paul said as much in the immediate context of Ephesians 3: "that you, being rooted and grounded in love, may have strength to comprehend with all the saints what is the breadth and length and height and depth, and to know the love of Christ that surpasses knowledge, that you may be filled with all the fullness of God" (Ephesians 3:17-19).

It's not normal to believe any such thing. It's certainly not normal for this to be the belief you hold deepest of all. Such a belief is divine. It's muscular. It's protein, not carbohydrate. It requires "strength to comprehend . . . the breadth and length and height and depth, and to know the love of Christ that surpasses knowledge" (Ephesians 3:18-19). What if we sought the pure strength to comprehend how inconceivably loved we are? What if we sought that love like the marvel it really is?

That strength isn't something we come to possess all on our own; it's a "strength to comprehend *with all the saints*" (emphasis added). We need other strengthened saints to remind us that we are loved beyond any human estimate of breadth, length, height, and depth. When those around us forget, they need our strength to remind them of this truth.

Amnesia is the inevitable infirmity of those who leave community. It's no accident that the call to sacred remembrance in Scripture is most often issued in the congregation.[1]

I'm still in the process of becoming deeply rooted and grounded in the love of Christ, but by His grace, I'm gaining strength.

Last year in a Q&A session, a young woman asked me a question I've reflected on a hundred times since. "Beth, what is the knot in your rope?" I'd never heard the question before. I knew my answer, but the thought didn't escape me how recently it had come to be so.

"It's John 15:9. Jesus said, 'As the Father has loved me, so have I loved you.'"

Christ loves us, just as God loves Him. When God quits loving Christ, Christ will quit loving you.

Till then, you've got a knot in your rope no demon in hell can hope to untie.

CHAPTER 14

alfresco

My earliest impression was that God was the indoors sort. Well, it was more than that. I figured God was a homebody, and it didn't help to clear up the matter that, the best I could tell from Sunday school, He spent all day in His robe.

Our church was God's house—a fact that couldn't have been good news to the Methodists and Presbyterians, who also gathered on Sundays, just down the street from where God lived at First Baptist. To be so close and yet so far away must have only salted the wound.

My family of eight piled into our blue and white Volkswagen bus and visited God at His house no less than three times a week, and I don't mind saying that I found Him there. The fact that He didn't go home with us was a fair assumption, based on the circumstantial evidence I witnessed behind our doors. I figured He stayed in the building all week long, lurking and lingering through the halls, ghost-like, sheet and all.

The baptistery at our church, which was perched right above the choir loft, held particular mystery to me, since the curtain stayed mostly drawn. For years, every time the preacher mentioned the veil in the Temple, I pictured it just like the beige polyester curtain that hung over the baptistery. With enough imagination, I could see the magical opening every time someone was baptized as a divine tearing, once removed.

In those days, we didn't get baptized over and over like people do now. Dr. Reeves held us under a good long time, speaking a few words to the congregation on our behalf. Coming up from the sacred waters, gasping for air, removed any substantial doubt that we'd been raised to new life. Of course, all this took place in what we now know was a hot tub.

To the question "Shall we gather at the river, the beautiful, the beautiful river?" we saints of yore replied, "No, we shan't. We shall gather in the sanctuary." And this was no crime. The Bible heralds an illustrious history of God blessing buildings with glory, and anyway, indoor baptisteries have cleaner water. Nothing is clean down by the riverside except the sinner willing to enter.

Jesus, the sinless Son of God, traipsed right onto the brown banks of the Jordan, robe and all, mud squeezing up through His toes. Perhaps He even stepped on the occasional sharp pebble as He headed toward a man who was waist deep in the water. This man was wearing a camel hair suit held on by a leather belt.

Those were strange times. Folks had been in and out of those same waters all day long, confessing and washing enough sins to drown a fish. There's no telling what was in those waters after that mass of humanity had stirred them up, but there Christ went, parting the waters that had led to the Promised Land, all subtle-like, with His own submerged body.

I don't have anything against coming up from the waters of baptism under the sacred blinding beam of a florescent light bulb. It still takes. After all, this is a work of the Spirit, not of the air. I only offer the elementary observation that Jesus put soles to the muddy riverbed and hair to the tadpoles, and He rose from those silty waters to the open skies. When He came up from the water, He saw heaven standing open and the Spirit of God soaring wide winged, southbound, diving like a dove straight toward Him. For an indoor kind of guy who mostly hung out at church, He certainly was outdoorsy.

✦ ✦ ✦

Most of Jesus' parables send us out of the house and into the elements. This is appropriate, since outside is where things grow best. Indoor parables are there for the taking in the sacred files, of course. The woman sweeping her house, looking for her lost coin, qualifies, but a woman with a broom in her hand more readily conjures up memories of my grandmother saying to us kids, "Scat outta this house 'fore I put you to work."

She'd point the bristled end of the broom right at us and glare down the handle, steely eyed, aiming that thing like a weapon. "I said *git*!" She'd do all this with a scowl on her face that we never took too seriously. But we ran anyway, as if she'd sweep the skin off our scrawny behinds.

The idea that God could have waited until the present to send His Son into the world is unthinkable for a host of reasons, but imagine the impact our present culture would have had on His stories. If He were to make examples of the everyday things we see, the woman could have swept the web looking for her lost Bitcoin.

I don't know what kind of discussions went on in the divine counsel regarding the timing of the Incarnation, but I wouldn't mind thinking that somewhere on the list of reasons not to wait until the twenty-first century was that the prospect of using parables found within the six inches between a human's nose and her cell phone gave Jesus the willies.

The first disciples didn't spend their days indoors in their underwear sharing the gospel on the Internet. I'm not saying that's a waste of time; it's not. I'm saying that as a regular routine, it would be a tragic waste of sunshine in the daytime and of sparkling stars at night.

In his book *The Art of the Commonplace*, Wendell Berry writes about the outdoorsy nature of Scripture:

> I don't think it is enough appreciated how much an
> outdoor book the Bible is. It is a "hypaethral book,"
> such as Thoreau talked about—a book open to the sky.
> It is best read and understood outdoors, and the farther
> outdoors the better. Or that has been my experience of it.
> Passages that within walls seem improbable or incredible,
> outdoors seem merely natural. This is because outdoors
> we are confronted everywhere with wonders; we see that
> the miraculous is not extraordinary but the common
> mode of existence. It is our daily bread. Whoever really
> has considered the lilies of the field or the birds of the air
> and pondered the improbability of their existence in this
> warm world within the cold and empty stellar distances
> will hardly balk at the turning of water into wine—which
> was, after all, a very small miracle. We forget the greater
> and still continuing miracle by which water (with soil and
> sunlight) is turned into grapes.[1]

Hypaethral basically means roofless. I live with a man who would choose "roofless" as his default setting whenever possible. I've fought a losing battle with a hypaethral man for the better part of forty years. Keith insists that the best church services he has ever attended have taken place when he was chest deep in a pair of waders while saltwater fishing.

In our early days of marriage, when I had more energy for shaming people, I'd ask him sardonically exactly what Scriptures were preached there. He would have an answer for me: "Follow me and I will make you fishers." Who among us has never abbreviated a Bible verse to fit our agenda? Let him cast the first stone.

Keith often retells a story about running his boat full throttle across the bay, the fiberglass base banging hard against the choppy waves. An ominous thunderstorm was blowing in, and he was trying to get to friendlier waters. He'd taken the boat out well before dawn that morning so he could be in his sweet spot for speckled trout when the sun rose. That lazy beauty should have been up by then, but instead, a storm came out of nowhere. Electricity filled the air as pellet-like raindrops assaulted his face. A cluster of thick, angry clouds burgeoned on the horizon, throbbing with lightning. Suddenly the center broke open, as if God had poked a hole through it, unleashing solar rays like spokes from a hubcap.

This is when Keith tells about the double rainbow that, for a matter of seconds, formed circles around the hole. His story has never changed, and the man isn't one to exaggerate, even when I think it might do a story some good. In particular, he's not one to make himself sound foolish. So if that's what he says he saw, that's what he saw.

He also says he brought the boat to a complete stop, and although it rocked recklessly with the buffeting waves, he held his hands straight up in the air. "So He could go ahead and take me," he explains every time. He pauses right there, picturing it all in his head, and then completes his thought. "I thought it was the Rapture."

Those kinds of things don't happen to you in the den while you're eating carryout on TV trays and watching season 5 of whatever. Those are the kinds of things that happen with the roof off. Certain brands of miracles are reserved for open cathedrals. They only happen *out there* in the elements.

Out there, we find ourselves under the stars that God calls by name, and we are made small against the expanse of the heavens. In awe, we whisper, "What is man that you are mindful of him, and the son of man that you care for him?" (Psalm 8:4). Only then can we embrace the wonder of the words that follow: "Yet you have made him a little lower than the heavenly beings and crowned him with glory and honor" (Psalm 8:5).

Out there, we discover that the fragrance of rain isn't the name of an air freshener. In the context of God's creation, our untested theories become absurdities and the six steps to success we've taught in our seminars fail us. Even the things we know to be true we share with humility, because we recognize that we all share the same humanity. We are all uninsulated and vulnerable.

Out there, sand and rocks are the only two options for building our lives upon. And our Maker refuses to force us to choose the rock. Out there, floodwaters rise and winds beat relentlessly against us. Out there, we plant seeds and then stare for days at the bare ground, wondering if anything at all will sprout and if a few dry days are signs of drought. Out there, we can't always tell the wheat from the tares. Out there, we can feel our hunger and thirst for something real, something whole—something that gets numbed indoors by cream soda and cheese puffs.

Out there, we're beaten up and robbed, lying on the roadside.

Out there, we're passed over and left for dead by people we expected to help us. Instead, to our great astonishment, we discover a neighbor in someone we thought was our enemy. Out there, we have an unobstructed view of the horizon, where we can spot the silhouettes of prodigals coming home. Out there, we can smell the sheep before we can see them. We can feel the sunshine after a cold, dark night. Out there, we discover treasures that are hidden in a field rather than in a safe deposit box. Out there, we see crosses being dragged through the dirt instead of hanging in sanctuaries.

When we're outside, exposed to the elements, we're reminded how little we really do control. We're hit afresh with the revelation that we're not as self-reliant as we thought we were. It's at once downsizing and upsizing. We can sense our smallness and God's vastness. It's not that we can handle our challenges indoors; it's that it's easier to believe our illusions of control. It's also easier to adapt to artificial light. Out in the wild, where we feel our smallest, our significance doesn't shrink. It swells. It is this very God who looks the world over to strengthen hearts committed to Him (2 Chronicles 16:9, NIV). It is this very God who plants roots in fields, not floors.

What I'm trying to say is that grapevines don't grow well in terrariums.

+ + +

We've become shut-ins, many of us—insulating ourselves to find protection from unprotected people and their endless predicaments, which shouldn't be our problem. Our wealth, relatively speaking, has afforded us the luxury of avoidance. Only a blind fool would romanticize poverty, and I will do no such thing, but a person who romanticizes prosperity is twice the fool.

God alone knows what our riches have stolen from us. The natural result of increased self-sufficiency is decreased God-dependency. Why would you need God if you're doing just fine on your own? On the playground of privilege, intimacy with the divine slips down the aluminum-smooth slide of self-reliance.

Attempting to find security in ourselves is fragile business, and much of the time, it's sheer illusion. We face one sizable crisis, and the bricks of our self-made house fall like toothpicks. There we are again, like most of the world, vulnerable to the elements.

By no coincidence, this is where our best productivity occurs. This is where we live and hear and see and share the gospel in earnest—as those who believe it and survive on it. This is where we are believable to the unbelieving. Until we get to that point, most of our talk is nothing but noise.

I despise a crisis as much as the next girl. I don't want one. I'm not asking for one. But we're talking about being immensely fruit-ful, and fruitful vines aren't houseplants. Let there be no misun-derstanding: profuse fruit bearing isn't crisis dependent. It's Christ dependent. But it's a rare follower who can indefinitely resist the lure of independence when everything is smooth sailing and not give in to its gentle lull.

The fact is, real beauty is found out there under the same sky as vulnerability. I'm not suggesting we can't die out there—we can. But we will most certainly die if we stay inside forever. Given enough time in the artificial light, within our insulated walls, our fruit will dry up and our branches will wither. Tap water simply can't compare with the feeling of rain on our faces. Hearing the wind is a paltry substitute for feeling it whip through our hair. Shut yourself in from the pain of exposure, and you'll also miss the sunset, where orange turns to purple and restores the souls of

REAL BEAUTY
IS FOUND UNDER
THE SAME SKY AS
vulnerability.

weary mortals. When we overinsulate ourselves, we're protecting ourselves right out of our callings.

Elijah the Tishbite tried insulating himself. He'd lived his whole life out in the elements. He'd seen fire fall from heaven. He'd seen Baal maimed and shamed. He'd seen a widow's dead boy raised to life. He'd sipped from a brook and been fed by ravens. He'd seen a drought begin and end as a result of his petition to heaven. He'd outrun a chariot at the sight of a fist-sized cloud.[2]

But then the unexpected happened. The triumphant Tishbite got bitten by the venomous threats of a bloodthirsty Jezebel. He fled to the wilderness and prayed to die. Thankfully, God knows which prayers are best answered with a hearty no. The man of God traveled "forty days and forty nights to Horeb, the mount of God. There he came to a cave and lodged in it" (1 Kings 19:8-9).

This scenario is tantamount to a master-class climber making it to the base of Mount Everest and then zipping himself up in a tent to sulk.

Better known as Mount Sinai, Mount Horeb was a national monument of sorts. In Moses' day, it was where the Lord descended, His glory wrapped in a thick cloud. It was where the Lord's fire blazed, lightning struck, thunder roared, and an unseen trumpet blasted. Elijah had come to Horeb, *the* mount of God. This wasn't a place where people sulked. This was the place where people shook. You don't travel forty days and forty nights to the mount of God to hunker down in a cave.

Have you ever gone to an immense amount of trouble to meet with God, and then, once you got there, you did everything on earth but actually meet with Him? And after all your self-distraction, you decided that God was the one who didn't show up?

Me, too.

Behold, the word of the LORD came to him, and he said to him, "What are you doing here, Elijah?" He said, "I have been very jealous for the LORD, the God of hosts. For the people of Israel have forsaken your covenant, thrown down your altars, and killed your prophets with the sword, and I, even I only, am left, and they seek my life, to take it away." And he said, "Go out and stand on the mount before the LORD."

1 KINGS 19:9-11

Go out and stand on the mount. Roofless.

There's no hiding from the One who covers Himself in garments of light. He's the reason you came, and you know it. He's the One you're mad at, and you know it. He's the One you somehow both want and don't want. And you know it.

Behold, the LORD passed by, and a great and strong wind tore the mountains and broke in pieces the rocks before the LORD, but the LORD was not in the wind. And after the wind an earthquake, but the LORD was not in the earthquake. And after the earthquake a fire, but the LORD was not in the fire. And after the fire the sound of a low whisper.

1 KINGS 19:11-12

If Elijah had remained inside, unexposed to mountain-tearing winds, crumbling boulders, quaking ground, and raging fires, who's to say he would have heard the sound of God's low whisper? Out under the big sky, where the wind howls and hisses, the Holy Spirit can also whisper.

The lesson of the vine and branch plants us outdoors again.

How perfect that Jesus taught this lesson outside in early spring, in the chilly night air of Jerusalem. There under a Passover moon and a canopy of stars He had called by name, God Incarnate made His way on calloused feet to a garden He had chosen.

How fitting that, in minutes, He would fall on His face in the dirt and, sweat pouring, make mud of it. He would cry out in near-death sorrow, "Abba, Father, all things are possible for you. Remove this cup from me. Yet not what I will, but what you will" (Mark 14:36).

Crucifixion was chosen as a method of execution precisely for its exposure. It was billboard torture—launched on a pole, high on a hill, where everyone could see. It was the Roman government's sermon on the mount, meant to incite fear not only of pain but also of public shame. Crucifixion was naked and raw, splayed and skinned. Crucifixion was out in the open sky. But the same open sky that exposed Jesus to the sight of commoners also echoed three words that would penetrate the highest heavens and save the lowest commoner's life.

It is finished.

CHAPTER 15

manure

Not everything unpleasant in the fruit-bearing process falls under the heading of pruning or even pestilence, as we will soon see. Some of it is just plain manure.

I love many things about Jesus, but the fact that He's the type to work a parable about manure into the Holy Scriptures rates right up there in the five-star bonus category.

Here's the story, according to Jesus.

> *A man had a fig tree planted in his vineyard, and he came seeking fruit on it and found none. And he said to the vinedresser, "Look, for three years now I have come seeking fruit on this fig tree, and I find none. Cut it down. Why should it use up the ground?" And he answered him, "Sir, let it alone this year also, until I dig around it and put on manure. Then if it should bear fruit next year, well and good; but if not, you can cut it down."*
>
> LUKE 13:6-9

The reader with a fine eye for detail may have caught the fact that the fig tree was in a grape vineyard and the tree tender was a vinedresser instead of an arborist. The fig tree's sense of place (terroir) may seem out of place to us, but according to Bible commentators, it was common to grow fig trees in vineyards.[1]

In fact, the combination of these two crops was idiomatic in the Old Testament for safety, personal well-being, and prosperity—the sort enjoyed in the reign of Solomon: "Judah and Israel lived in safety, from Dan even to Beersheba, every man under his vine and under his fig tree, all the days of Solomon" (1 Kings 4:25).

A hundred years after Solomon, the children of God were on the precipice of disaster, about to reap what their unabated waywardness had sown. The prophet Micah foretold sure woes for the Israelites, along with exceedingly great mercies.

> [The Lord] shall judge between many peoples,
>   and shall decide disputes for strong nations far away;
> and they shall beat their swords into plowshares,
>   and their spears into pruning hooks;
> nation shall not lift up sword against nation,
>   neither shall they learn war anymore;
> but they shall sit every man under his vine and under his fig tree,
>   and no one shall make them afraid,
>   for the mouth of the LORD of hosts has spoken.
>
> MICAH 4:3-4, EMPHASIS ADDED

The promise of fruit from the vine and the tree wasn't just about food. It was about hope. It offered thriving evidence of a destiny fulfilled. It meant that the land, the grape plant, and the fig tree were doing what they were created to do: produce fruit.

Just shy of the end of the Old Testament, the prophet Zechariah referenced the messianic era, when God would remove the sins of the land. "In that day, declares the LORD of hosts, every one of you will invite his neighbor to come under his vine and under his fig tree" (Zechariah 3:10).

In God's economy, what good is prosperity if it isn't shared? Divine vitality breeds hospitality, and hoarding is appallingly unholy. To love self without loving neighbor is to know nothing at all of the love of God.

When Jesus told the parable of the fig tree midway through Luke's Gospel, He turned up the volume on the vinedresser's patience and compassion. He earnestly desired to delay judgment so he could work with the tree and urge it to fruitfulness. If, after the determined length of time, the tree still didn't produce anything, he'd agree to the brisk swing of an ax.

Commentator Joel B. Green says that this parable is striking because it "holds for the possibility of fruit-bearing in spite of a history of sterility—or, in human terms, the possibility of change leading to faith expressed in obedience to God's purpose. If it announces a warning of judgment, then, it also dramatizes hope."[2]

The possibility of fruit-bearing in spite of a history of sterility. Those are spectacular words, aren't they? That means our histories don't get to impose themselves on us like prophecies. We don't have to be who we've always been. Whether we've had four years of spiritual sterility or forty, that blockage can be removed. We can embrace a new pattern of abiding, and the life force of the Spirit can flow through our branches, making us astoundingly fruitful.

This is the grace of God. This is the transforming power of the Cross. This is the way of the God of countless chances.

But the Vinedresser reminds us that we don't have forever. We don't even always have long. We only have now. We only have this slender slice of time.

NOBODY TOLD ME A
PRODUCTIVE LIFE
WOULD INVOLVE
QUITE SO MUCH

manure.

"Give me a little while," the Vinedresser says, "and let me dig around in it and put some manure on it."

The wording in the King James Version is especially fun, if you ask me. But then again, I've been married to Keith Moore for an undeniably long time.

He answering said unto him, Lord, let it alone this year also, till I shall dig about it, and dung it.

LUKE 13:8, KJV

Dig about it and dung it. That should do the trick.

+ + +

Don't dream that the Vinedresser won't dig around in your well-manicured soil. He doesn't even mind tearing up your landscaping, if that's what it takes. He won't just go digging up your old skeletons and unearthing a few fossils of your family tree. He's liable to dig up all sorts of things that got buried alive.

Let's get down in there and see why you're not growing, he says. Let's find out why your fruit is stunted.

Oh, don't think He won't. But if He does, you need not wonder why. The Vinedresser digs around the roots of a tree to stimulate fruit, to prod and goad that plant into productivity, to shock it a bit with a shovel so it will wake up and do what it's meant to do.

He also fertilizes it with manure.

Nobody told me a remotely productive life would involve quite so much manure. That's why I'm telling you. If you want to live an immensely fruitful life, you will have to deal with substantial piles of it. I wish I could tell you otherwise, but we both know better.

From my personal experience and observation, there are plenty of people willing to provide the manure for you. You don't have to go out looking for it; it will find you. Sometimes it's just a shovelful here and there, and other times you'll feel like a truck just unloaded on you.

This is the stuff in our lives that stinks to high heaven—stuff we feel like we shouldn't have to put up with but we must. If such is common to man—and unfortunately, it is—then such is compost to fruit-bearing man. And woman.

Don't get me wrong. I'm not saying you have to like the manure. It is, after all, dung. But what you can come to appreciate is that the Vinedresser can use it as potent fertilizer toward some fine fruit in your life. The manure bearer—a donkey, let's say—isn't meaning to do us any favors. It's just doing what it does and passing on what it has eaten. (This is as good a time as any to remember that people dish out what they consume. We can't tell them what to eat, but we can watch our own diets.)

The gardener can take what is nothing more than a pile of putrid manure, apply it to the base of our tree, and do us an enormous favor.

At first, the manure that gets heaped on you will appear to have no value at all. You won't seem to learn a thing from it except perhaps that people can be cruel. You'll go through an ordeal or an attack, an assessment or a critique that even years later you will think had no constructive element whatsoever. It just seems meaningless.

But it's not. It's manure. We need a name for it, and that's as fine a one as I've found.

People will say inexplicable things. They'll do inexplicable things. Some things won't make a whit of rational sense—but they will make good manure.

I don't know if this is of any help to you, but it's done a world of good for me, so I'm passing it on, just in case. The next time you're faced with an unpleasantry that seems to possess no real value, even after prayer and good, stiff self-evaluation, it might be of comfort to file it away in the manure category.

While the following musings are admittedly better left unsaid, imagine redirecting your mental responses in ways like these:

> *I'm pretty sure you just meant to be mean,*
> *but what you did might fertilize my tree.*
> *So thank you. God bless you.*

> *Based on your tireless disparagements, you*
> *seem intent on getting me to quit, but instead*
> *you very well may have added to my longevity. Think*
> *how your heaps of manure could stimulate my fruit.*
> *Thank you. God bless you.*

I'm thinking you get the idea by now, but in case you could use one more, here's a handy one:

> *That is truly one of the rudest things I've ever*
> *heard, but eureka! What rich fertilizer!*
> *Thank you! God bless you.*

Perhaps, like me, you might even dream of sending a case of fig preserves to someone as a thank-you.

Even manure matters. And that's a good thing, because let's face it. Manure happens. But it need not be all waste.

CHAPTER 16

pestilence

Only one thing attracts the attention of the devil like the smell of blood. It's the smell of grapes.

There is a coming-of-age for healthy branches (and you know by now that when I say *branches*, I'm referring to fruit-bearing Jesus-followers). This coming-of-age isn't so much about the passage of time, as if the hands of a clock alone could dictate the maturity of the plant. At some point in your growth in the faith, you will face a drought or a plague or a blight of some kind. That's when you will discover what your fruit is made of—and if it can withstand the elements that rail against it.

Of course, anyone can face the threat of losing it all, but I'm specifically talking to those who are doing what it takes to bear fruit for the gospel and paying the price. I'm talking to those who are in this Jesus-serving thing up to their necks, whether in secular or religious spaces.

More pointedly, these words are to you if you're coming of age in your calling, even if, like me, you're not even sure how you got here most of the time. Oh, you could try to tell someone younger in the faith what steps you took. You could post a blog about it. You could do an effective Q&A on the topic. Perhaps you could even write a decent book about it. But deep in your heart you know that much of the time, you really had no earthly idea what you were doing.

At the end of the day, all you can say is that you kept doing *something—the next thing—to serve Jesus,* however awkwardly and, in hindsight, perhaps embarrassingly, you pulled it off. But lo and behold, something finally started working. Not all the time, of course, and not flawlessly, but satisfyingly enough to suggest that you might be on to something. Your works started producing some semblance of fruit, and you have a sense that you're where you're supposed to be for now.

Unless we're bitten by rabid self-ambition, our contribution doesn't have to be big. All our meaning-craved souls really need is for it to be fulfilling, to feel like we're actually working with God instead of trying to coax Him into working with us.

But this coming-of-age isn't typically marked by a personal sense of thriving. Rather, it's marked by a harrowing suspicion that somebody out there hates you. Somebody . . .

big
and powerful
and vicious
and patient
and deceptive
and mean
and alluring
and beautiful
and terrifying
and knowledgeable.

Somebody who has your personal information—or, to be more direct, somebody who knows your secrets. What may be less obvious is that this being is far more concerned about your successes than your secrets. Your effective fruit bearing imposes the biggest threat to his agenda. His primary interest in your secrets is in leveraging them most effectively to stifle, smear, or stop your successes.

If the devil is doing his best work, you will think the somebody in question is God. There will be times you're convinced to your bones that God Himself is opposing the very thing He called you to do. Rather than believing that the One who called you is faithful to perform it (1 Thessalonians 5:24), you may feel like the One who called you is systematically, frustratingly *keeping* you from performing it.

You might be tempted to think that God tricked you into something and then refused to support you. Or that He talked you into something beyond your natural abilities and then abandoned you, leaving you to fend for yourself.

When the devil is doing a superb job, you may feel like God called you and then changed His mind about you, as if He didn't know who He was getting when He chose you.

If this reads like your present season, it's likely you are awakening to the war. Your eyes just haven't adjusted to the darkness yet. See if any of these statements have a familiar ring to them:

You didn't know serving God would be like this.

When you surrendered to Jesus, you had no idea what you were stepping into.

You figure you must have done something wrong for it to be this hard. It wasn't like this when you started.

You must have been too prideful. Maybe you enjoyed serving too much.

Your previous fruit must have all been a fluke. You're a one-work wonder.

You're too embarrassed to tell anyone about the battle you're in. They'll think you brought it all on yourself.

What you may not realize is that every other person worth his or her salt in the Kingdom either has gone through their own version of the same thing or is enduring it this very minute. And it's hellacious.

✝ ✝ ✝

With the first scent of ripe, plump grapes, the devil comes like pestilence. Of course, you may not call it spiritual warfare yet, because that's what the older generations called it and you want to be cooler than that. But after sufficient time in the trenches, I can all but promise you that coolness will be a casualty of war.

Until you make it through several seasons of severe pestilence, where worms, bugs, spiders, and rot attempt to devour you, you can go on your merry way, half convinced that the devil is not that real. Not that specific. Not that personal. Not that plugged in. Not that in tune. The devil is simply the way the Bible personifies darkness, you reason. Anyway, if he turns out to be more than that, there's no way God would let him mess with your calling or your kids.

If you want to hold on to that fantasy, skip over the book of Job, flee from the Psalms, and run for your life from Esther.

The coming-of-age battle isn't limited to external forces like pestilence sent from the belly of hell. Satan can conserve significant energy if we'll simply enlist as our own worst enemy. This is good old-fashioned autosarcophagy: the practice of devouring one's own self.

MUCH OF THE WAR
AGAINST THE DEVIL
IS ABOUT WHETHER
you'll quit.

When we turn the attacks inward, our vulnerabilities and our impressive abilities start erupting into liabilities. Our own hands take a crowbar to every crack in our armor. We're tempted to do things we swore we'd never do and things we've publicly judged others for doing. Our past comes calling.

If you're single, the challenges you've navigated with minimal effort before now loom over you like a tidal wave. Methods you've sworn by and shared with others no longer seem to be working. If you're married, your marriage, which you've boasted about publicly, now looks like it's about to go up in smoke. If you're a parent, your kids, who up until now have been obediently fulfilling your own dreams and making you tremendously proud, look like they're coming unhinged. The remarkable blessings of God on your job, your serving life, or your ministry now seem bafflingly absent. Your rising star feels like a sinking stone.

Half the time, you may think you're losing your mind, and you hope nobody has noticed. You're getting criticized. You're attracting a lot of opposition. You daydream about quitting and moving to a remote island, wearing loincloths, drinking milk out of coconuts, and swimming with dolphins. At night, you have nightmares that you hung in there in your calling and it slaughtered you.

Congratulations. You have come of age.

What you're going through is how it goes for nearly everyone who's serious about serving Jesus. Now that you've come of age and had the faith and the audacity to bear much fruit, you have come of notice to the devil. Simultaneously, your unstoppably faithful God, who loves you immeasurably, has made a covenant at the Cross not only to save you but to conform you to the image of His Son.

Out of His exquisite grace, His obligation is to grow you up.

And there is anguish in growing up. Among other things, growing up forces us to face the deceiver and pretender in our own mirror.

If this is the season you find yourself in, I can fairly confidently assure you it won't always be this brutal. It will always be hard. At times it will be horrific. But this season of eye-bulging, *nobody-ever-said-it-would-be-like-this* pestilence won't last forever. Mine lasted roughly seven years. Since that time, I've had numerous other seasons that were equally hard, but I'm no longer naive, unarmed, and unprepared.

More important, some matters got settled that first time around. Part of growing up is settling some things. Settling some things from your past, for instance, and landing with resolve on some decisions you've gotten away with being noncommittal about in the past. Settling some things can mean mustering the courage to draw a line that you know deep inside needs to be drawn. For me, growing up was fueled in part by being burned by my own duplicity. As I looked back at the trail of ashes I left behind, I made up my mind about who I wanted to be and then stuck with it.

Your coming-of-age amid a harrowing pestilence might not last as long as mine did. That's all up to God. Well, God and you. Your cooperation is required. If you never learn to fight, you can be a soldier, but you can't be a warrior.

The motto of the inexperienced is "Ignore the devil, and he'll go away." Nobody says that after a bloodbath. James says it this way: "Resist the devil, and he will flee from you" (4:7).

That's how this works. *Resist* is no passive term. It stands its ground, steel toed. It pushes back. It shoves hard. It applies divine might—a coat of armor, a sword in the right hand, and a shield in the left.

Much of the war against the devil is about whether you'll quit.

Or whether you'll get sloppy. Or whether you'll hang on to what drove you in the beginning:

Jesus.
Scripture.
Godly passion.
Holiness.

And it's not just about hanging on to these things but about pressing further into them, with fresh faith. Questions like these have particular relevance in the culture surrounding us: Will we resolve to do what it takes to become a bona fide, tested-and-tried disciple of Jesus Christ—bearing what we have to bear, learning what we have to learn, denying what we need to deny, and embracing all there is to embrace? Or will we slip into the seductive black hole of busyness and business, platform and position, notoriety and name making, marketing, carnality, self-importance, celebrity, and branding?

After the fiercest battle of your life, when you are no longer naive, what will you do? If you let yourself and others down—at some point, we all do—will you give up, believing the lie that you no longer have what it takes? Will you just go with the current and figure degeneration naturally follows regeneration? Or will you fight to get a pure heart back?

The sobering words of Galatians 3:3 come calling. Will you try to do in the flesh what you began in the Spirit? Will you leave praying up to "prayer warriors" so you can avoid the trouble of laying it all out on the floor before the Lord? Will you delegate to someone else the fight for the ground God entrusted to you? Or will you fight with everything you've got until you're bloody and bruised?

I know these questions by heart, because I've used them on myself.

+ + +

Coming of age is the most critical intersection of your calling. It's the place of Spirit and slaughter. It's the corner where you take one of two turns: either your fruitfulness will be devoured by the devil or your own flesh, or you will allow God to crucify your ego, fear, and lethargy and raise you to be immensely fruitful for His gospel.

If you're in a season of pestilence, fight it out. If you've gotten sloppy, tighten it up. If you're neck deep in sin, repent. Go back on your face before God. Open a Bible and plant your nose in it. Memorize Scripture. Learn how to fast and pray. Quit talking about Jesus more than you talk to Him. Quit letting your mouth overshoot your character. Become that person you've made fun of for taking Jesus too seriously. Live and love valiantly. Give generously. Help the poor.

You'll come out on the other side of every well-fought fight with something far better than an immense quantity of quality fruit. You'll come out knowing Jesus in a way you formerly believed He couldn't be known.

Jesus Himself is the prize, preeminent in all things. Fellowshipping in His sufferings, delighting in His presence, growing in His grace, experiencing His power in weakness, discovering His peculiar peace in chaos, and finding comfort in His consolations—these are the prizes that make the furious battle worth fighting.

One of these days, when we get to talk with Jesus face-to-face and recount to Him how the pestilence nearly destroyed us, He might tell us, perhaps with a smile, that our souls were never at risk—and, really, neither was our fruitfulness. He never took His eyes off of us. He never left us on that battlefield alone. He fought for us. He defended us. He took the assaults against us personally. He did for us what God did for Joseph in Genesis 49:24. When the demonic archers came for us, shooting bitter arrows, He caused our bow to remain steady, and our "arms were made agile by the hands of the Mighty One of Jacob."

Jesus knew how things would play out. He knew what we had in us when the devil came after us. He put it there Himself.

That's why you were allowed to be tested almost beyond what you could bear. He knew you'd prove genuine. Even when we feared we were fakes, Jesus knew better.[1]

PART 5

The Harvest

On this mountain the LORD Almighty will prepare
a feast of rich food for all peoples,
a banquet of aged wine—
the best of meats and the finest of wines.

ISAIAH 25:6, NIV

CHAPTER 17

ingathering

In the small-town church I grew up in, I would have been able to tell you a lot of words that describe God's character. In the verses I memorized and the sermons and Sunday school lessons I sat through, I learned that God is holy. He is eternal. He is all-powerful. He is good. I believed He was nice. But if someone had asked me if God was happy, I would have suddenly gone mute, as if I'd been thrown a trick question.

I was acquainted with a fallen world before I even knew what a bra was. I would have wondered how in heaven's name God could be happy, as horrible as humans were. As horrible as *I* was.

I was well into the throes of adulthood before I discovered that God is indeed a God of joy. This was no emotional epiphany—my feelings would have been the last thing to convince me. I came to accept divine joyfulness because Scripture referenced it over and over again.

"Joy cometh," the psalmist said in the King's English, and he was right (Psalm 30:5, KJV). It always does. "Weeping may tarry for the night," sang this poet who was no stranger to tears. "But joy comes with the morning." The promise holds true even when the dark night tarries into weeks and months. Even when suffering seems to last the larger slice of a lifetime. And weeping won't simply be relieved at the break of the eternal day—it will be utterly displaced by joy.

Despite messages we may have heard to the contrary, ours is a God of great joy. In the parable of the talents, Jesus used that one word to characterize our whole future with Him. The servant's welcome at the door of heaven is an ode to joy: "Well done, good and faithful servant. . . . Enter into the joy of your master." In John 15, home to the teaching of the vine and branches, Jesus said, "These things I have spoken to you, that my joy may be in you, and that your joy may be full" (John 15:11).

"My joy," Jesus said, "in you."

The Man of Sorrows was simultaneously the Man of Joys—in ways perhaps beyond our comprehension but not entirely beyond our experience. As I try to grow a vineyard from ground to ripe grape in the soil of my imagination, I've explored many of the hardships and challenges of preparing a vineyard. But I have a hunch I may have underestimated just how joyful cultivation can be.

+ + +

Imagine that it's dawn, and you and I have just pulled up to a vast, green vineyard on a rolling hillside. The grapes are at peak ripeness, shimmering in the dew. It's basket-grabbing season. But lest you slog onto that field heavy footed, looking like your dog just died, you need to know that the harvest is boisterous. The work is hard, but the mood could hardly be lighter.

After all the laboring, rock clearing, hoeing, weeding, waiting, growing, staking, guarding, pruning, weather watching, and clock watching, the time has finally come for grape picking. And as it turns out, with grape picking comes partying. I don't just mean there's a party at the end of the picking, although that's true, and it will hit fever pitch at that point. I mean there's partying in the midst of the picking. I couldn't be more pleased.

Partying was God's idea. He strung festivals like holiday lights into the annual Hebrew calendar—seven in number, each commemorating His faithfulness, and He commanded His people to celebrate them. Three of these were pilgrimage feasts, trumpeting Israelites throughout the land to come up (always up, never down) to Jerusalem.

> *Three times in the year you shall keep a feast to me. You shall keep the Feast of Unleavened Bread. As I commanded you, you shall eat unleavened bread for seven days at the appointed time in the month of Abib, for in it you came out of Egypt. None shall appear before me empty-handed. You shall keep the Feast of Harvest, of the firstfruits of your labor, of what you sow in the field. You shall keep the Feast of Ingathering at the end of the year, when you gather in from the field the fruit of your labor. Three times in the year shall all your males appear before the Lord GOD.*
>
> EXODUS 23:14-17

The viticulturist's eye is fixed on the festival at the end of the year: the Feast of Ingathering, also called the Feast of Tabernacles or the Feast of Booths. The Israelites who made the trek camped all over Jerusalem in small booths or huts they erected from palm branches. These booths were reenactments of the temporary shelters the Israelites had built during the forty years they traversed the desert.

More to our present point, the booths were also the same kinds of shelters set up by ingatherers during the harvest season. By God's good pleasure, He calendared this official celebration at the tail end of the grape harvest.

Feast on the joy God assigned to the occasion in Deuteronomy:

> *You shall keep the Feast of Booths seven days, when you*
> *have gathered in the produce from your threshing floor and*
> *your winepress. You shall rejoice in your feast, you and your*
> *son and your daughter, your male servant and your female*
> *servant, the Levite, the sojourner, the fatherless, and the*
> *widow who are within your towns. For seven days you shall*
> *keep the feast to the LORD your God at the place that the*
> *LORD will choose, because the LORD your God will bless*
> *you in all your produce and in all the work of your hands,*
> *so that you will be altogether joyful.*
>
> DEUTERONOMY 16:13-15

Altogether joyful.

Time was of the essence for the ingathering. Wait even a few days too long, and ripe grapes start to wither and rot, skins popping, splitting, or shriveling. The Israelites had to move fast, and the bigger the vineyard, the more laborers were required. Entire villages were often involved in the picking, and booths pocked the vineyard's edge.

Men, women, and children moved rhythmically up and down the rows, baskets in hand, singing, dancing, and rejoicing. They shouted to one another over splendid clusters, celebrating with unbridled conviviality the goodness of God in bringing fruit from the dust of the earth.

Everyone was invited to participate. "The rejoicing community included family, servants, widows, orphans, Levites, and sojourners."[1] The only ones left out were those who refused to join in. "You shall rejoice in your feast," they'd been commanded. Laugh and carry on. Whistle while you work. The Lord has dealt bountifully with you (Psalm 13:6).

The exuberance carried over from the grape clipping in the vineyard to the grape stomping in the winepress. "He will shout in triumph like those stomping juice from the grapes" (Jeremiah 25:30, NET).

Maybe I'm making too much out of it, but imagine the reduction in pent-up anger we'd experience if we could throw ourselves into an annual festival of shouting and grape stomping. "The celebrations were so much a part of the vintage that if they were absent, it would be seen as a mark of God's judgment."[2]

These lines from Isaiah put the conspicuous absence of harvest celebrations into sorrowful lyrics:

I drench you with my tears,
*   O Heshbon and Elealeh;*
for over your summer fruit and your harvest
*   the shout has ceased.*
And joy and gladness are taken away from the fruitful field,
and in the vineyards no songs are sung,
*   no cheers are raised;*
no treader treads out wine in the presses;
*   I have put an end to the shouting.*

ISAIAH 16:9-10

In other words, God intended joy to be such a part of the harvest that, if it was missing, the people of God would know something was awry. Sustained joylessness was a red flag, an indicator for them to raise their chins and look to God for what had gone wrong.

The problem wasn't always direct disobedience. Sometimes an oppressive enemy was to blame. Either way, joy was never meant to be a hit-or-miss condition of the people of God. Joy was divinely determined to be one of a believer's most consistent and distinguishing features.

+ + +

When my girls and I were in Tuscany at the end of the harvest, we arranged for a cab to take us to Siena for a day trip. Our taxi driver wound us down the hill from our lodge, turning onto a two-lane road where a dozen cars were parked on its bone-thin shoulder.

I was spellbound by the sight of harvesters walking the vineyard rows—nearly waltzing, in my romanticized recollection—with baskets and clippers, reaping the fruit from the final few acres. By the time we returned from Siena six hours later, not one cluster could be found.

Dates for the harvest are set depending on numerous variables. Vineyard management pores obsessively over weather forecasts, watching for any extremes predicted at peak ripeness. Heavy rain, hail, frost, and smoke are wicked foes to the vintage, so under imminent threats, the harvest may be gathered early to cut the losses. The vineyard chemist is also on high alert, testing samples for acidity and sugar levels.

Before long, ready or not, the reaping begins. Volunteers show up before dawn, fill out the proper forms, and gather around a vinedresser for scrupulous training on how to eye a desirable cluster and cut away what is rotten. The workers are then marshalled forth like troops for the great ingathering, clippers in one hand and a container in the other. They are ready to carry out one of the richest traditions observed for millennia.

To be sure, most vineyards around the world have moved to machinery for the picking, but each harvest site I toured still reaped grapes the old-fashioned way. Delightfully, many vineyards, even those in Texas, still invite people from nearby communities to participate.

The ingatherers, who were strangers to one another on their arrival, are fellows by the time of their departure. They have labored together, boasted of beautiful grapes together, and bemoaned what was tragically rotten together. They have eaten together, both lunch and dinner—the latter of which can be quite the spread.

Then the party rises to its peak. The way each vineyard parties is up to the owner, but let us not assume that the divine vineyard Owner and His Vinedresser would expect their workers to abstain from rejoicing. In fact, celebrating is something we do *because* we're made in God's image.

When Jesus told the parable of the Prodigal Son, He gave us one of the dearest, most treasured of all illustrations of God as Father. Maybe some people get tired of hearing it, but to those of us who have been neck deep in the pigsty, the story never gets old.

The father welcomes a sin-sick, self-shamed son back home where he belongs. Nothing is vaguely subtle about the reception. We see no private reintroduction to his home. There's no family meeting to agree on the version of the story to tell in town. The father instantly throws a party with music so loud and dancing so boisterous that the older brother can hear the sounds reverberating

Partying

WAS GOD'S IDEA IN

THE FIRST PLACE.

through the walls and raising the roof as he returns from the fields (Luke 15:11-32).

Despite the reputation of many believers, Christian virtue is not marked by a quickness to bemoan and a reluctance to rejoice. The opposite would come closer to the truth. It's not a badge of maturity to sit back passively and refuse to take joy in our fruitfulness. We're meant to celebrate and kick up our heels a bit when the Lord of the harvest brings fruit from our labors. When we act as if we don't notice God's blessings, it's not humility. It's ingratitude.

I have to believe this is part of the reason community is such a vital part of the harvest. The group effort involved in the ingathering provides a built-in temperance for the individual ego. In the presence of co-laboring, egos shrink.

Autonomy, a value so prized and awarded in our culture, has made the body of Christ sick. We are bleeding our joy, stifling our songs, and muffling our laughter. Our self-reliance has kidnapped us and left us stranded on the shores of microscopic one-man islands.

Instead of embracing our identity as sons and daughters of the Vinedresser, we live as resentful hired hands. Our eyes shift frantically up and down the vineyard rows, jealous of those whose baskets appear to have more fruit than we do and judging those whose baskets appear to have less. We forget that we were meant to work together, feast together, mourn together, and celebrate together. These are the birthrights we've been given as children of God.

+ + +

I've waited all this time to point out when the first vineyard shows up in Scripture. You'll find it no later in the canon than Genesis 9.

The sons of Noah who went forth from the ark were Shem, Ham, and Japheth. (Ham was the father of Canaan.) These three were the sons of Noah, and from these the people of the whole earth were dispersed.

Noah began to be a man of the soil, and he planted a vineyard.

GENESIS 9:18-20

Nothing will make you a man of the soil like tossing for weeks on water. You get the idea that Noah had barely lost his sea legs when he started hoeing the ground. I wish the text would linger there awhile so I could hear all about how Noah searched for a fertile hill and cleared it of stones and built a watchtower and all. However, God was particularly sparing with words when He inspired this segment of Noah's story. The text moves straight from "he planted a vineyard" to "he drank of the wine and became drunk and lay uncovered in his tent" (Genesis 9:21).

The proximity of these two verses could leave a reader thinking that Noah climbed right off that boat and got summarily plastered. You might even wonder if anyone could blame him. However, now that we've accrued a few lessons in viticulture, we know that by the time Noah had planted a vineyard, reaped a harvest, and made the wine, months, if not years, might have passed since his disembarkation.

There's no need to cover for Noah. Shem and Japheth saw to that (Genesis 9:23). Noah was a righteous man, and new to viticulture, after all. But I have to admit it's not the way I would have scripted the scene.

Still, maybe the scene that's being scripted isn't altogether different from the world we live in. We were meant to bear an immense amount of fruit and find gladness of heart in it, but we weren't meant to get drunk on it. Our platform-driven culture runs rife with people who are drunk on their own fruit, intoxicated by attention.

That's not the way God intended it. Extravagant joys can abound in community, as long as we don't succumb to big egos, petty rivalries, and our own insecurities. In fact, I'd go so far as to say that we who are in Christ are never happier than when we're celebrating a harvest in community.

When the Holy Spirit is abundant and active in us, we don't care much who has gathered the most fruit at reaping time. We were all part of the vintage year, moving up and down those rows together at the Feast of Ingathering. The credit for a great harvest goes to the Vinedresser, but the glee abounds to all.

Altogether joyful.

"These things I have spoken to you, that my joy may be in you, and that your joy may be full."

In his commentary on this verse, Dr. Leon Morris makes a point I find fascinating. Up until the farewell discourse on the evening of Christ's arrest, the Gospel of John records the word *joy* only a single time (John 3:29). Then, on that final evening, Jesus goes on record using it an undeniably deliberate seven times. It's like fireworks.

Morris writes, "It is no cheerless, barren existence that Jesus plans for his people. But the joy of which he speaks comes only as they are wholehearted in their obedience to his commands. To be half hearted is to get the worst of both worlds."[3] I deeply believe this to be true. We resist offering ourselves wholly to anyone or anything that has the potential to encroach on our personal desires, and Jesus made clear from the start that God's will and ours would be in conflict at times. Yet our surrender to Jesus is also ultimately our surrender to joy.

Dr. Morris quotes another scholar, Dr. R. H. Strachan, with words I find irresistible: "The *joy* of Jesus is the joy that arises from the sense of a finished work. It is creative joy, like the joy of the artist. It produces a sense of unexhausted power for fresh creation. This joy in the heart of Jesus is both the joy of victory ([John] 15:11), and the sense of having brought His church into being."[4]

The joy of the artist. Is it any wonder that artists throughout time have drained paint buckets brushing vineyards across canvases? And what is it that causes a personless landscape captured in manmade acrylics to awaken the romantic in us?

It's not just the hope of a table set with crystal glasses. The magic happens long before then. Perhaps somewhere deep in our imaginations, we paint in the people. We know inherently that no vineyard grows itself. No harvest gleans itself.

With your mind's eye, go ahead and stare into that painted landscape for a while, and then read between the lines of the vineyard. Those are no bare rows.

See, oh seer, the reapers in the fields, robes blowing in the breeze, baskets in hand. Children are running, laughing, chasing, tagging. Men and women are clipping, waltzing, filling, carting. Hear, oh hearer, the songs, the joyful shouts, the sounds of gleeful celebration.

It is the holy feast of the happy ingathering, the dance of God and man.

CHAPTER 18

gleanings

God has His own way of doing things, a fact made as clear as a crystal chalice by the work ethic He assigned for the fruit harvest. He taught me the lesson in living color while we were in Tuscany.

When my daughters and I returned from our day trip to Siena, I was flabbergasted to find every branch in the vineyard completely cluster free. The grapes were in their season finale, and the reapers we'd spied were snipping the last few rows. By the time we headed back six hours later, they had long since waltzed their way home.

The branches were now fruit bare, and the rows were as clean as freshly swept kitchen floors. I remember this detail with particular clarity, because the fruitless vines have been the topic of a good bit of razzing between my daughters and me.

Early that morning, enthralled by the sight of the grape harvest in progress, I'd hastily unsnapped my seat belt and summoned the taxi driver to pull over so I could take pictures of the reapers with my phone.

As the driver steered toward the shoulder, the girls chimed in with immediate protests. "Mom, wait until we're on our way back!"

I protested but was outvoted three to one, the driver eying them affirmatively through the rearview mirror.

Instantly the girls resorted to oath taking. "We promise we'll stop this afternoon!"

Don't imagine their reasoning was entirely about getting to Siena on time. My daughters know their mother, and they predicted an enthusiastic spectacle at the vineyard, complete with large blonde hair, copious gestures, and cheers of "*Ciao!*" in such a multisyllabic Southern drawl that the driver would have had to translate. Though I'd like to think the reapers' joy would have been complete with my drop-by, the girls were less convinced.

I also had lofty notions—dreams, really—about how spectacular my pictures would be. They could have turned up in a travel magazine, for crying out loud. "What an eye Beth has," people might have said. I could see the whole thing in my head. Never mind that it takes me no less than twenty shots to get a decent picture of a plate of enchiladas for Instagram. This could have been my big break. Alas, I emerged from that fateful day bereft of a single picture. But had I been transported in time to an earlier era, afoot a road beside a Judean vineyard, none of this would have happened. Why? The vineyards would not have been swept completely clean. God said so—and not just once.

The first mention of this commandment is in Leviticus:

When you reap the harvest of your land, you shall not reap your field right up to its edge, neither shall you gather the gleanings after your harvest. And you shall not strip your vineyard bare, neither shall you gather the fallen grapes of

your vineyard. You shall leave them for the poor and for
the sojourner: I am the LORD your God.

LEVITICUS 19:9-10

Several chapters later, the same instruction is repeated:

When you reap the harvest of your land, you shall not reap
your field right up to its edge, nor shall you gather the
gleanings after your harvest. You shall leave them for the
poor and for the sojourner: I am the LORD your God.

LEVITICUS 23:22

The command to leave margin at the edge of the field is given
again, most powerfully, in Deuteronomy:

You shall not pervert the justice due to the sojourner or to the
fatherless, or take a widow's garment in pledge, but you shall
remember that you were a slave in Egypt and the LORD your
God redeemed you from there; therefore I command you to
do this.
When you reap your harvest in your field and forget a
sheaf in the field, you shall not go back to get it. It shall be for
the sojourner, the fatherless, and the widow, that the LORD
your God may bless you in all the work of your hands. When
you beat your olive trees, you shall not go over them again.
It shall be for the sojourner, the fatherless, and the widow.
When you gather the grapes of your vineyard, you shall not
strip it afterward. It shall be for the sojourner, the fatherless,
and the widow. You shall remember that you were a slave in
the land of Egypt; therefore I command you to do this.

DEUTERONOMY 24:17-22

"Remember where you've been," the Lord commanded, in essence. "Remember the rock from which you've been hewn. Remember that I redeemed you. You didn't do this for yourself. You have been the wanderer. You have been the dependent, cast upon on the mercy of strangers who owed you nothing. In your privilege, don't dare to overlook those without it."

Sit awhile with the most striking feature of God's commandment in both passages. The leftover fruit wasn't to be left haphazardly here, there, and yonder. The Israelites were to leave it on the edges, where it would be most accessible for those who needed it.

Human nature being what it is, the Lord's people would have more likely left the fruit in the center, where it would have been most difficult to gather. "Let them do the part we don't want to do." As God often does, He called His people to a reversal of natural tendency—both as a service to others and as a way to set them apart from the world. "Make it easy for those in need. Make their provision plain to see."

✦   ✦   ✦

Early one harvest many centuries ago, the breath of the Spirit blew over the barley fields of Bethlehem. It brought the law to life through real people, with real names and real futures at stake.

Here is the scene: A young woman named Ruth walks away from her home in Moab to join her mother-in-law, Naomi, on an onerous journey northward to Bethlehem, the older woman's homeland. Both women are widowed and sonless and, as such, in dire straits. But their plights are far from equal. Ruth enters the Judean scene doubly disadvantaged as a Moabite, a foreigner.

Upon arriving in Bethlehem, their survival is dependent on meeting an imminent need. They have to eat, and in order to keep eating, they have to find a way to sell a parcel of land that was still in the name of Elimelech, Naomi's deceased husband. "So [Ruth] set out and went and gleaned in the field after the reapers" (Ruth 2:3).

Most of us don't live close enough to a barley field to know where our bread comes from. If that's you, allow me to expound on a basic harvesting term. You might think of gleaning as gathering information little by little. But in the ancient Judean world, gleaning was an agricultural term that referred to the gathering of grain left behind by the reapers. For the disadvantaged, this God-crafted custom carried the weight of life and death on its back.

Gleaners and reapers were by no means peers in the ancient world. Gleaners came in behind the reapers to gather whatever produce was left in their wake. They would need permission to gather the leftovers from a landowner's field, so they were dependent on finding someone with compassion—or at least someone who feared God.

Herein lies the tension of the book of Ruth. A landowner named Boaz sees a young woman gathering ears of grain left behind by the reapers and inquires about her. Note how her foreignness is mentioned twice in the reaper's reply, lest Boaz miss it: "She is the young Moabite woman, who came back with Naomi from the country of Moab" (Ruth 2:6).

Large-hearted Boaz invites Ruth to glean exclusively from his fields, and then he goes a step further. He uses his authority and privilege to see to it that she is not harmed. "Have I not charged the young men not to touch you? And when you are thirsty, go to the vessels and drink what the young men have drawn" (Ruth 2:9).

When mealtime comes, the plot thickens like heavy cream. Boaz invites Ruth to share his bread alongside the reapers and dip it into the house wine. She takes her seat beside the reapers, and the roasted grain passes from his hands to theirs and then to hers, apparently escaping no one's notice. When Ruth rises to return to her gleaning, he promptly awards her increased access to his field.

> *Boaz instructed his young men, saying, "Let her glean even among the sheaves, and do not reproach her. And also pull out some from the bundles for her and leave it for her to glean, and do not rebuke her."*
>
> RUTH 2:15-16

The ink draws a rapid bond between Ruth and Boaz, lassoing the couple in a clandestine scene at the threshing floor, where hopes of marriage are exchanged at the Cinderella stroke of midnight (Ruth 3).

As in any truly great story, a threat arises to their union. A closer relative than Boaz has the legal right to redeem the land and marry Ruth to perpetuate the family name and claim the inheritance (Ruth 4:5). To the reader's relief, this man declines, and Boaz assumes the role of kinsman-redeemer.

Wedding bells ring, and the Moabite widow becomes the bride and the landowner becomes the rich of heart. The story ends epically, with the new couple's son cradled in the grandmother's lap. Call Naomi bitter no longer.

They name the child Obed. Obed grows up and fathers Jesse. Jesse grows up and fathers David, who grows up and takes the throne of Israel. Several centuries later, David has a descendant named Joseph. Joseph is betrothed to Mary, who gives birth in Bethlehem to the Son of the Most High, conceived by the Holy Spirit. Jesus directly descends from the line of a kinsman-redeemer, a Bethlehemite named Boaz and a Moabite woman he met gleaning his field.

Maybe you're familiar with Ruth's new mother-in-law's name. It's Rahab (Matthew 1:5). The story could hardly be more superb, nor the lineage more significant. Is it any wonder Joseph was the kind of man he was? The belief in new beginnings was in his blood.

What Ruth sought to glean was barley so she could put food on the table. She was driven by her immediate need: a meal. What she ultimately received, however, was more than she could have dreamed. She was given a second chance. New life. Redemption. Grace. A place in the most important lineage in human history.

Take a look at the edges of our fields, and you'll see people our society claims don't matter. But in God's eyes, every soul is of inestimable worth. And these people at the edges of the field are hungry. Hungry for love. Hungry for affection. Hungry for friendship. Hungry for a listening ear. Hungry for hope. Hungry to know God is there and that He cares. And I wonder—have we harvested with the margins in mind? Do we intentionally serve people on the edge?

We have gleaned such grace from the Vinedresser's field. "Freely you have received," Jesus said. "Freely give" (Matthew 10:8, NIV).

+   +   +

John's Gospel tells us that "the law was given through Moses" and "grace and truth came through Jesus Christ" (John 1:17). But lest the graced ones misinterpret these words, grace didn't break the law of Moses, like stone tablets thrown into worthless fragments. Grace loosed the law of love from its limits.

This truth is vividly illustrated in Jesus' parable in Luke 10:25-37. A teacher of the law tries to corner Jesus by questioning Him about eternal life. Jesus masterfully steers the conversation so the lawyer publicly recites the royal law of love toward God and neighbor.

Relishing the microphone, the self-justifier then asks Jesus the million-dollar question: "Who is my neighbor?"

So, Jesus, just how far does this love thing go?

Suddenly, the listener—let's just say it's you, for now—is transported into the story. You become the unsolicited lead, traveling a notorious road from Jerusalem to Jericho in the Jordan Rift Valley. Your footsteps quicken, sandals slapping the dirt. You kick up dust as you make your way from 2,500 feet above the sea toward the Jordan, some eight hundred feet beneath it.[1]

They're on you before you know it. You're not sure how many of them there are, but there are enough to engulf you. Enough to block the sun. Enough to render what feels like a hundred blows.

"Here, take the coins!" you plead, digging for the pouch in the folds of your garment. But they don't stop until they take your clothes, too. Your body rolls like a rag doll as they jerk your robe out from under your back.

You're sure you'll die there. You breathe shallow breaths, because a broken rib has nearly pierced one lung clean through. Through the slits of your swollen eyelids, you see someone coming down the road. Thank God, it's a priest—a descendant of Aaron. You can tell by his clothes. You try to move your mouth to make some kind of sound. Nothing comes out. But he sees you. Thank God, he sees you.

Then his steps swerve to avoid you. He's tired, you know, and anxious to get home after serving his shift in the Temple. Status can be grueling.

By now the blood from a head wound is making mud of the dust beneath your cheek. You blink, trying to remain conscious.

Then another form appears on the road. Another man of

notable piety. Wait—does he think you're dead? Is that why he's passing on the other side? Is he afraid you're unclean?

You try to stir. You moan. You think he hears you.

He picks up the pace.

You shut your eyes to die. Someone is carrying you—an angel, perhaps. Maybe this is how death goes. Your eyelids are caked shut.

Your body is lowered onto a blanket. A stream of warm water pours over your hair and then runs in rivulets down your face.

You feel the towel—soft, gentle, daubing. You hear a voice murmuring words of compassion. You smell the oil and the wine. One hand slips under your head, the other wraps it with gauze. Around and around, easy does it. You're dizzy and nauseous, but you try to speak. You want to ask, "Do I know you?"

"Rest," he says.

When you return to consciousness, you hear two voices. The first one says, "Take care of him. Whatever you spend, I will repay you when I come back." You try to place the accent. You know it doesn't belong to anyone you know, to anyone you've ever wanted to know.

The other voice consents.

You don't fully awaken until hours later, when the innkeeper checks on you. "The Samaritan says he'll be back," he says.

Samaritan. You've never even said the word without spitting. You stare at the ceiling, absorbing the shock, the scent of oil and wine lingering.

Jesus interrupts the scene playing out in your imagination. "Which of these three, do you think, proved to be a neighbor to the man who fell among the robbers?"

Playing the part of the young lawyer, you say all you can say: "The one who showed him mercy."

Jesus says to you, "You go, and do likewise."

+ + +

It may be fair to say there's never been an envelope of any consequence that Jesus didn't enjoy pushing. He pushed this one too, unwilling to draw the line, even at the extreme of loving unliked neighbors.

> *You have heard that it was said, "You shall love your*
> *neighbor and hate your enemy." But I say to you, Love your*
> *enemies and pray for those who persecute you, so that you*
> *may be sons of your Father who is in heaven. For he makes*
> *his sun rise on the evil and on the good, and sends rain on*
> *the just and on the unjust. For if you love those who love*
> *you, what reward do you have?*
>
> MATTHEW 5:43-46

Love God.
Love one another.
Love your neighbor.
Love your enemy.

That about covers it. In Christ's meticulous census, the community exempt from the love of Christians has a population of exactly zero.

"But Lord, what about . . . ?"
Love them.
"But those wicked . . . ?"
Love them.
"But those hateful . . . ?"
Love them.
"But those unbelieving . . . ?"
Love them.

ONLY GOD CAN

save the world.

BUT WE CAN SERVE

IT A FRUIT PLATE.

And this isn't just about giving lip service to loving other people. Jesus isn't impressed by love in word but not in deed (1 John 3:18). In Jesus' reckoning, when it comes to love, confession without action is pretention. To Him, the distance from hype to hypocrisy is a slippery inch and a half. When we do take action, but mostly for the sake of being seen, He's uninterested in rewarding the show (Matthew 6:1-4). Jesus simply can't be played.

However, Jesus is perfectly eager to reward faithfulness. Throughout the New Testament, He has sprinkled promises of rewards for loving as He loved, serving as He served, giving as He gave, and forgiving as He forgave. And what goes unrewarded in our temporal lives will be rewarded in our eternal lives and enjoyed forever. He just doesn't stomach pretension well.

Love God. Love people. That's what we're here to do. "The fruit of the Spirit is love" (Galatians 5:22). Without love, all fruit is plastic. The fruit of our lives, in all its forms and manifold graces, is truest to the Vine when it's generously extended and accessible to strangers and aliens of any kind.

Our fruit is sweetest to the Vine when it extends a direct advantage to the disadvantaged and to the orphan, to the widow and to the poor. Our fruit best reflects the Vine when it deliberately leaves room at the edges—for the marginalized, the cornered, the oppressed, the mistreated, the harassed, and the abused. That's where Jesus went, and that's who Jesus sought. "As he is so also are we in this world" (1 John 4:17).

The challenging part is that none of this fruit is a bargaining chip to win the gleaner's evangelization. It's free. No strings attached. There for the taking. Simply put, we're meant to be agents of good in the world, not professional closers for Jesus. But make no mistake: when we endure and do good, *that* will witness.

Nothing is more important than people coming to Jesus, but only the Spirit can bring them. I believe in eternal life, in heaven and in hell. I believe Jesus alone is the way, the truth, and the life. I believe we're each called to share our faith. I believe the mission of the church is to go to the ends of the earth.

But no one is won to Christ in a bargain.

✝ ✝ ✝

My beloved older brother is Buddhist. In case you're wondering if it's a passing phase, he has been one for forty years. He is a brilliant man who has spent his entire career in the world of musical theater. Early in his work in New York City, he and his wife were introduced to Buddhism and embraced it.

I've been reluctant to put much about his beliefs in writing out of my protectiveness toward him. Frankly, I don't want Christians, even well-meaning ones, to harass, befriend, or exploit him in an effort to convert him. He's too smart for that, and nothing could be more counterproductive.

In fact, it was well-meaning harassment that sparked a hostility between us, shutting down all but surface-level communication for years. A family member had a faith awakening, and he fixated on my brother's conversion. I knew it wasn't going to go well, but the fallout was worse than I feared. One day he announced to me—and I knew he meant it—"I'd rather go to hell than for him to be right."

In an effort to spare our relationship, we decided to take all discussion about religion off the table. This went on for years. The problem was that our spiritual beliefs are so integral to our lives that dodging them became stiff and awkward and turned each of us into parodies.

My big brother and I are kindreds. Our personalities are compatible. Our tastes are similar. We love poetry and music and discovering new restaurants and recipes. He loves cooking, and I love eating. We have the same taste in novels and movies. We're fine with talking and fine with silence. We're amused by the same absurdities. But somewhere along the way, many of our commonalities got lost in the wash of our contrasts.

On the phone one day, wearied by our self-imposed boundaries, I said, "I want to learn about what you believe. What books would you recommend to me?"

That day the walls started coming down. Over time, we freed each other up to talk just as we would to anyone else. No rules. No awkwardness. I mention Jesus in our conversations with him, just like I would with anyone else. He refers to chanting and what he's doing in his Buddhist community, just like he would with anyone else.

Over the last few years, he has watched my attempts, as inadequate as they are, to speak up against sexism and misogyny and racism and white supremacy. He knew my convictions came directly from what I believe about Jesus and the Scriptures. He saw the backlash of criticism my outspokenness caused and reached out to me sympathetically. It came as an eye-opener for him when I explained that at least I wasn't alone in this and that a growing number of Christians with similar convictions were becoming more vocal.

He hasn't embraced Christianity, but I can tell you this: he no longer thinks Jesus is a jerk. God help me, I can't help but think that's progress. In the past, he viewed Christians, particularly evangelicals, as the most self-serving people on the globe, out only for our own agenda. What spoke loudest to my unbelieving brother was that Christians were taking action in a way that wasn't self-serving. He was surprised to discover that the fight for justice represents no departure from our Christian doctrine. In fact, this fight springs directly from what we believe.

In a society that's increasingly populated by "nones" (those claiming no religious affiliation), Christians have increasingly responded by pulling toward the poles of either dead silence or loud defensiveness. But there's another way. It's possible to love in deed and do good to others, neither flaunting nor hiding our identity. We are the people of Jesus, the One who said, "This is to my Father's glory, that you bear much fruit, showing yourselves to be my disciples" (John 15:8, NIV). We are not called to be showy, but make no mistake: we are called to be showing.

Peter knew what it was like to build the church in jeopardous times. He also knew what to do amid a vast landscape of nonbelievers:

Maintain good conduct among the non-Christians, so that though they now malign you as wrongdoers, they may see your good deeds and glorify God when he appears.
1 PETER 2:12, NET

God wants you to silence . . . foolish people by doing good.
1 PETER 2:15, NET

Let those who suffer according to the will of God entrust their souls to a faithful Creator as they do good.
1 PETER 4:19, NET

In his letter, Peter acknowledges a significant reversal. He and his fellow Jesus-followers had become the "foreigners and exiles" (1 Peter 2:11, NET). Fruit is stockpiled to the skies in our Christian communities. We have enough gifts, enough abundance, to fill the arms of untold gleaners at the edges of our fields. Does the Old Covenant exceed the New Covenant in compassion? The Cross makes such a prospect preposterous. Has our freedom in Christ set us free from the law of loving our neighbors and the foreigners among us? Of course not. Are we off the hook from protecting the vulnerable and the exposed? Not a chance.

The truth is, we're not so far removed from Boaz. We have the divine lineage of the kinsman-redeemer running through our veins.

Deep inside, we all want to do good to other people. We know that we, too, were once wanderers. We, too, were once slaves. We, too, were once poor in spirit. But now, in Christ, we have found a home. We have been set free. We have been made rich.

We may not be owners, bosses, or managers, and we may not be wealthy or well known, but we possess more authority than we recognize. We put it to use in our neighborhoods, in our children's schools, in our churches, in civic matters, in social issues, and on social media. Any place we have influence, we utilize a measure of authority.

If we're exercising this authority as imitators of Christ, we don't do so as bullies who are strong-arming others in the name of Jesus. Rather, we're acting as influencers of good, identifiable by the kindness of Christ. We may not see the likeness of Boaz in the mirror, but we resemble him every time we use the authority and influence God has entrusted to us to extend our advantage to the disadvantaged and to protect those who are vulnerable to mistreatment and abuse.

Take a fresh look at your fields. There at the edges you'll see gleaners. Once your eyes adjust, you can no longer *unsee* them. Some of us have been raised in our churches and theological circles to fear the very world Christ told us to invade with His gospel.

I'm not suggesting that we aren't at risk of having the world rub off on us. We are. But maybe it's time to rethink our misguided motto, *Never cater to the world.*

If Boaz was anything at all in the book of Ruth, he was a caterer passing around a fruit plate. Maybe catering to the world is exactly what we should dare to do—but not with carnality, coolness, or compromise. The world doesn't need more worldliness. It needs sustenance.

Only God can save the world. But we can serve it a fruit plate. Cater on.

CHAPTER 19

feast

Supper is almost ready.

I'm not a great cook. This is no false humility, because I am,
as a matter of fact, a formidable baker. But I'm a merely passable
cook. The only reason some of my family members might argue
with this self-assessment is because these days I stick mostly to
what I stir up well.

Cooking is primarily a means to an end for most of us. But for
me, on the occasions when I enjoy it most, the end game isn't a
full stomach. It's a loud family comprised of multiple generations,
sitting around my dining room table. It's a cross section of the
same blood, whether they were born into it, married into it, were
welcomed into it, or were dragged into it.

It's those people who pass around the yeast rolls and say, "Who's
hogging the butter?" It's sitting between grandchildren and knowing with unshakable confidence that the moment Willa gets tired

of what's on her plate, she'll get down from her booster chair, crawl into my lap, and eat what's on mine. It's knowing that she's going to make such a mess of the green bean casserole that it will be unrecognizable mush in less than a minute, and I'll need to make another plate behind her back.

On big holidays, I like to write out a schedule on the marker board in my kitchen with the exact timing, down to the minute, for everything from taking the meat out of the refrigerator to making the tea, slicing the lemons, and filling the glasses with ice. I love most of all when we're about an hour out and my people start bursting through the door like calves breaking out of stalls. I love hearing raucous rounds of, "Man, something smells so good!"

What I lack in cooking skills I make up for in garlic.

I hug each person tight then point them to the appetizers on the kitchen counter. They're always simple ones—usually crackers and cheese or chips and salsa. If you asked my people if they wished we sat down at the table the second they walked through the door, the adults would all say no. You know as well as I do that a certain amount of anticipation is as essential to the brimming pleasure of a great meal as the actual consumption. One reason we want to know the menu in advance is to get our taste buds primed and ready for it.

+ + +

Jesus isn't one to depreciate the value of anticipation for a fine meal. "I have eagerly desired to eat this Passover with you before I suffer," He said to His disciples just hours before His arrest (Luke 22:15, NIV). That Jesus could think about savoring anything, knowing what He had coming, is a testimony to His otherness.

Scripture gives no indication that Jesus picked at His food that night, but it does point to something fascinating regarding a certain kind of fasting. I'll pull the lens back a bit so you can see the point in context.

When the hour came, Jesus and his apostles reclined at the table. And he said to them, "I have eagerly desired to eat this Passover with you before I suffer. For I tell you, I will not eat it again until it finds fulfillment in the kingdom of God."

After taking the cup, he gave thanks and said, "Take this and divide it among you. For I tell you I will not drink again from the fruit of the vine until the kingdom of God comes."

LUKE 22:14-18, NIV

Let this be no small consolation to those who, for any reason, choose to abstain from wine. You need not be ashamed among those who are free to partake. As it happens, you're in good company. In anticipation of future events, Jesus apparently chose the final meal before His death as the moment to begin a period of abstinence Himself.

A number of Scriptures assure us of meals in the next life. I won't act like I'm not relieved about this revelation. Some of us might argue that heaven could hardly be heaven without food, but we don't have to speculate. Word of one great banquet is leaked to us in the New Testament:

I heard what seemed to be the voice of a great multitude, like the roar of many waters and like the sound of mighty peals of thunder, crying out,

"Hallelujah!
For the Lord our God
the Almighty reigns.

Let us rejoice and exult
    and give him the glory,
for the marriage of the Lamb has come,
    and his Bride has made herself ready;
it was granted her to clothe herself
    with fine linen, bright and pure"—

for the fine linen is the righteous deeds of the saints.

And the angel said to me, "Write this: Blessed are those who
are invited to the marriage supper of the Lamb." And he said
to me, "These are the true words of God."

REVELATION 19:6-9

How sublime of Jesus to choose the apostle John to record these words so near the close of the canon. It seems like a fitting way to bring the idea of a divine wedding feast full circle, since the opening miracle in John's Gospel took place at the marriage in Cana. For the beloved disciple, wedding banquets were bookends to an age—at one end, the Bridegroom's glory revealed, and at the other, His bride's role fulfilled.

"Blessed are those who are invited to the marriage supper of the Lamb."

It's a true story. John assured us of that when he wrote, "These are the true words of God" (Revelation 19:9). We will attend a wedding feast to exceed all wedding feasts, even the famous one in Cana. We will rejoice and exult, John says. And after all our self-awareness and self-consciousness, don't tell me that exulting won't be refreshing. I know some uptight people I'd like to catch in the act of exulting. Of course, I'll be sweet about it by then. I'll be happy for them. I'll be happy for myself.

We're going to be happier than we can imagine. We'll have to be, in order for Paul to reckon under divine inspiration that "the sufferings of this present time are not worth comparing with the glory that is to be revealed to us" (Romans 8:18). Only a fool would deny that the sufferings of this present time are titanic and demoralizing.

I have a friend who has had twelve miscarriages. The happiest married couple I know moved into a brand-new home a few months ago. When the husband set down one of the last boxes in the shiny new entryway, he looked a bit flushed, his brow damp, so his wife went to fetch him a glass of water. By the time she returned with it, he was absent from his body and present with the Lord—just like that. I recently prayed for a young woman, mighty in faith, who had just been diagnosed with the recurrence of brain cancer. She wants to keep living here, on this disgruntled sod we constantly complain about.

We don't realize what we have coming in the next life. I don't think we're meant to. If we truly grasped the magnificence of what's ahead, we'd be too anxious to leave.

Paul got a glimpse of where we're going, and he testified to the conundrum. No translation of Philippians 1:23-24 competes with the King James Version, so bask away in it: "I am in a strait betwixt two," Paul wrote, "having a desire to depart, and to be with Christ; which is far better: nevertheless to abide in the flesh is more needful for you." Sometimes we people of faith wonder why we're so prone to squirm through life on this earth. It's because we're in a strait betwixt two, that's why. It gets tight in here.

I think God gives us occasional inklings of how happy we'll be when we're united with Him. We experience punctures in this bubble of temporal madness—times when eternal bliss seems to bleed through. These quick bleeds of bliss are unpredictable. If they weren't, we'd expect them to show up at every significant human experience, like graduations, births, baptisms, and award ceremonies. If your experience is similar to mine, however, these glimpses of fleeting, otherworldly bliss tend to appear in ordinary moments, when you let down your guard.

+   +   +

I'd be remiss to end this book without telling you that Keith and I have a new puppy. Another baby bird dog, white with three brown swaths and countless freckles. She has elephant ears and gigantic paws just like her predecessors, who tore up our yards and then tore up our hearts. Keith named the other dogs after rivers. This one is Creek, plain and simple.

As we sat on the front steps, watching her run and roll and tumble in our grass, that bouncing ball of speckled fur suddenly stopped dead still and went on full point. She was straight as an arrow from the tip of her nose to her cropped tail, locked on a bright yellow butterfly.

We laughed as if we didn't have a care in the world, as if we couldn't feel the first breezes of winter against the north sides of our faces, as if it hadn't been close to a year since the coyotes ripped the life out of our nine-year old, one-eyed bird dog that we loved to no end.

A butterfly doesn't have a brain much bigger than a pinhead, but as I live and breathe, I'm convinced that insect made a game of it. It flitted and flirted with our tiny bird dog like a crayon-yellow Tinker Bell, swooping down to land on her nose and then, while Creek snapped at the air, mischievously darting up again.

Creek broke point and leaped in the air repeatedly to catch the pair of wings. That puppy came as close to a pirouette as any four-pawed creature you've ever seen. For just a moment, Keith and I had an inbreak of bliss, full and fat as homemade peach ice cream, reawakening the hearts of two people who haven't had the luxury of ten minutes in a fairy tale world to believe that, somewhere over the rainbow, skies *are* blue. In that eternal, cloudless day, there exists a world we'll finally call perfect.

I think laughter is audible hope. It's wordless, of course, as it ought to be—perhaps because it speaks a language we do not yet know. We're more resilient than we should be, and I mean this about far more serious things than the loss of a dog. I don't know many people of generous age who haven't suffered something big enough to knock the laughter out of them for life.

But more often than not, sooner or later, a laugh erupts from our chests—and ordinarily over nothing significant. It's not what we laughed about, after all. It's that we laughed, right here in the same air as our despair. It's that our insides betrayed a hope, as well masked as it may have been.

Hope doesn't happen in a vacuum. There's a hidden knowing inherent in hope. In order to exist and persist, hope knows something real, however faint it may seem That knowing is what we call faith. And faith is not wispy. It's no wishing upon a star. It is a white-knuckle conviction of what we cannot see.

We know a better world is coming, though we don't know when and though even the best theologians can't explain exactly how. We know an eternal God won't stop until He has brought everything full circle. We know because He said so. As surely as God redeemed humans from the curse of sin through the Cross, He will redeem the earth from the curse of sin that caused the ground to rebel against the work of human hands.

God alluded to that day long ago through the prophet Hosea. He describes the coming of the Kingdom, when wars will cease

LAUGHTER IS

audible hope.

and peace will reign. He quotes God, saying, "I will betroth [my people] to me in righteousness and in justice, in steadfast love and in mercy. I will betroth you to me in faithfulness" (2:19-20).

In that day I will answer, declares the LORD,
I will answer the heavens,
and they shall answer the earth,
and the earth shall answer the grain, the wine, and the oil,
and they shall answer Jezreel,
and I will sow her for myself in the land.
And I will have mercy on No Mercy,
and I will say to Not My People, "You are my people";
and he shall say, "You are my God."

HOSEA 2:21-23

This dance of answering is mesmerizing. God will answer the heavens, the heavens will answer the earth, and the earth will answer the grain, wine, and oil. And the grain, wine, and oil will answer "Jezreel!" meaning "God will sow."

This was the prophet's poetic way of expressing uninterrupted responsiveness—all things working together as they were originally intended to. No more frustration. No more thorns growing where we thought we planted corn.

Likewise, the massive and masterful book of Isaiah draws toward a close with these lyrics concerning a new creation:

Behold, I create new heavens
and a new earth,
and the former things shall not be remembered
or come into mind.

But be glad and rejoice forever
in that which I create;
for behold, I create Jerusalem to be a joy,
and her people to be a gladness.
I will rejoice in Jerusalem
and be glad in my people;
no more shall be heard in it the sound of weeping
and the cry of distress. . . .
They shall build houses and inhabit them;
they shall plant vineyards and eat their fruit . . .
and my chosen shall long enjoy the work of their hands.

ISAIAH 65:17-19, 21-22

When I came upon these words in my search of the Bible's references to vineyards, I stared at them for the longest time. Right there in the Old Testament context of a brand-new creation, where people could have ready-made food of the finest order, God curiously references the planting of vineyards. Why on earth would planting be necessary in a perfect world? One glorious explanation is that God's delight is not just in the fruit; He's not interested in results alone. He elates in the entire process of fruit bearing. He relishes the mirthful participation of His image bearers, the Imago Dei, in a divine work. A sublime work.

The New Testament ends with a slightly different angle in its description of a new heaven and earth, with her brilliant New Jerusalem. The tree of life, introduced in Genesis 2, is showcased in the final chapter of Revelation. It has been perfectly planted beside the crystal-clear river of life flowing from the throne of God.

Here's a particularly wonderful part of the scene: the tree of life is described as "bearing twelve crops of fruit, yielding its fruit every month" (Revelation 22:2, NIV). This isn't instant fruit, appearing out of nowhere; rather, the tree bears fruit each month. God can bring about fruit any way He wants to, and in the glorious forevermore—in that sweet by-and-by, when we meet on that beautiful shore—what He wants is an unceasing rotation of fruit bearing.

God likes watching things grow.

And so do we, but it's fair to say there's one thing we like more than growing: eating. "Blessed are those who are invited to the marriage supper of the Lamb" (Revelation 19:9).

After all Isaiah has sung to us throughout these pages, it seems fitting for him to sing one last song. There's no putting this one to a country tune, like we did with his song of the vineyard in Isaiah 5. This one calls for soaring choral music along the lines of Handel's *Messiah*:

> *On this mountain the LORD Almighty will prepare*
> *a feast of rich food for all peoples,*
> *a banquet of aged wine—*
> *the best of meats and the finest of wines.*
> *On this mountain he will destroy*
> *the shroud that enfolds all peoples,*
> *the sheet that covers all nations;*
> *he will swallow up death forever.*
> *The Sovereign LORD will wipe away the tears*
> *from all faces;*
> *he will remove his people's disgrace*
> *from all the earth.*
> *The LORD has spoken.*

In that day they will say,
"Surely this is our God;
  we trusted in him, and he saved us.
This is the LORD, we trusted in him;
  let us rejoice and be glad in his salvation."
ISAIAH 25:6-9, NIV

No more death. No more disgrace. No more tears. No more shrouds. This description sounds a lot like the ending of Revelation, supper and all. If the two passages are talking about the same point in time, we have the richest of foods and the finest of wines coming. Maybe I'm wrong, but I suspect the wedding supper recorded in Revelation 19 is when Christ will pick up His glass again (Luke 22:17-18).

"The kingdom of heaven is like a king who prepared a wedding banquet for his son," Jesus taught in one of His parables (Matthew 22:2, NIV). One day all of us who are in Christ will gather around enormous tables exquisitely set with an extravagant feast prepared in divine kitchens.

No one will be left out.
No one will be alone.
No one will be nameless.
No one will be unknown.
No one will have nowhere to go.
We will finally be home.

✝   ✝   ✝

My friend Susan says that whatever heaven is like, it will be the best possible everything. She says this to all sorts of questions, like

"Will dogs go to heaven?" and "Will there be little children?" and "Will we get to eat cheese?"

"I have no idea," she responds, "but this you can count on. God will see to it that it's the best possible everything."

I don't think God minds supposition, as long as we call it that. I'll tell you how I picture the scene. The glasses are poured—by angels, perhaps—and not a single hand of the recipients will go over the rim of a goblet to forbid it. It will be too late to abstain. Too late not to celebrate. Too late to make a mess of things. Too late for tipsy. Exultation will have taken tipsy's place.

In my mind, John rises from his chair to propose a toast—John the Baptist, I mean. I think it has to be him, because he's the official "friend of the bridegroom" (John 3:29), and in the tradition I know best, the best man is in charge of the toast. Maybe he clinks the glass to get the attention of all the gatherers in the banqueting hall.

I find the thought that the Baptizer might be picking up a wine glass for the first time particularly delicious. Not a drop touched his lips during his lifetime, when he devoted himself to making people ready for the Lord (Luke 1:15).

Of course, he might have been greeted with a celebratory cup soon after he got to heaven, but I figure that if Jesus abstained until the Kingdom had fully come, John would be the type to join Him.

We all get to suppose our own stories. And we'll all aim too low anyway, because the actuality will far surpass our fanciful thoughts. But attempting to imagine can blow away cobwebs and breathe some fresh life into our religious lulls. Whatever we have coming, it will be the best possible everything.

"All rise," I imagine John saying, and of course we will. "I'd like to propose a toast."

We'll reach for our goblets and raise them high.

"Cheers and eternal hallelujahs to our Champion, our King, the Lord of all lords, the holy Lamb of God."

We will roar like those who have been tutored in voice lessons by the Lion of the tribe of Judah. Then, all together, from the Head of the table to the tail, we will tip the cup and sip the gift of our heavenly Canaan's grapes. The Master of Ceremonies, true to His form in John 2, will have saved the best wine until now.

In the words of author Robert Capon,

> Water come of age . . .
>> To Wine indeed
>> To Water *in excelsis.*[1]

Jesus will look upon those He was pierced for and for those He was crushed for, and see "a great multitude that no one could number, from every nation, from all tribes and peoples and languages" (Revelation 7:9).

His Father, too, will gaze upon the sight. There in the banqueting hall at the great and glorious feast, the eyes of God will roam the heavens as they have roamed the earth. And peering down lengthy tables protracted like branches, alive and abiding, He will behold the fruit of the Vine.

> *In that day,*
> *"A pleasant vineyard, sing of it!*
>> *I, the LORD, am its keeper."*
> ISAIAH 27:2-3

Take heart, Jesus-follower, in this dry and weary land. Serve with abandon. Supper is almost ready.

EPILOGUE

You could say that I started chasing vines in Tuscany in the back seat of an Italian taxi. But in reality, I started chasing vines way back when I was nine years old, sitting in the church pew in my patent leather shoes.

My soul felt the call of the vineyard and the divine Vine long before I knew to put it in those words. I just knew I wanted to be part of something grander than my own ordinary existence. I wanted my life to matter.

Many years have passed since then, but in some ways not much has changed. I still want something that makes everything in my life matter—the agonizing parts and the glorious parts and everything in between.

And I wonder . . . how did it all start for you? When did you start chasing vines? When did you begin dreaming that one day you might be chosen for something bigger than this life? When did you start hoping that you could be part of God's matchless plans?

+ + +

I'm fairly certain we won't need taxis in heaven. But if we did, I imagine Jesus might meet you at the gates, throw His arms around you, and then hop into the cab with you for a retrospective tour of your life.

The way I picture it, you'll watch everything biography-like, seeing the highlights and the lowlights through redeemed eyes. Jesus will point out the window and say, "See that rocky patch over there? The rough terrain that tore the soles from your shoes and left your feet black and blue? It was part of making you into the person you are now."

You'll pass by a place you lived for a spell, a place you never would have chosen if it had been up to you. "That spot was no accident," He'll say. "You were right where you were supposed to be. In fact, that was sacred ground."

He'll pull over at a field to let you get a close-up look at the soil. He'll show you how deep your roots went—deeper than you ever would have imagined. And while you're poking around in the dirt, He'll show you how the dead things were actually part of the humus of your life.

Then He'll take you on a series of stops to look back on the most excruciating scenes you endured. The place where you were pruned within an inch of your life. The place where pestilence nearly finished you off. The place that was heaped with more manure than you could throw a pitchfork at. But this time you won't see the pruning shears or the blight-eaten leaves or the dung pile.

You'll see only the beauty that came from ashes, the joy that sprung out of mourning, the praise that grew out of the soil of despair.

He has sent me to tell those who mourn
that the time of the LORD's favor has come. . . .
To all who mourn in Israel,
he will give a crown of beauty for ashes,
a joyous blessing instead of mourning,
festive praise instead of despair.
In their righteousness, they will be like great oaks
that the LORD has planted for his own glory. . . .
Instead of shame and dishonor,
you will enjoy a double share of honor.
You will possess a double portion of prosperity in your land,
and everlasting joy will be yours. . . .
The Sovereign LORD will show his justice to the nations of
the world.
Everyone will praise him!
His righteousness will be like a garden in early spring,
with plants springing up everywhere.

ISAIAH 61:2-3, 7, 11, NLT

Finally Jesus will show you a field with basket upon basket of plump ripe grapes. "Where did this harvest come from?" you'll wonder.

The Vinedresser will grin from ear to ear. "This is the fruit of your life. You know how I like to make things grow."

Then He'll put His arm around you. "There was never a moment I wasn't with you. I was singing over you the whole time."

That's the curious thing about chasing vines. Somewhere along the way, we discover that the Vinedresser has been chasing us all along.

And He makes everything matter.

ACKNOWLEDGMENTS

Writing requires an enormous amount of time in solitary confinement, but publishing takes a team. Thirty years into this profession and almost as many books, I am blessed nearly to tears to make the honest claim that I've never once had a team I didn't love. Let me save you the energy of jumping to the conclusion that I must be easy to please, because I'm not. I fairly naturally like people and relish working elbow to elbow on projects, but I can be embarrassingly stubborn. I've had great teams because I have a very gracious God. I'm so, so thankful.

The team involved in this writing project is large enough to roll up dozens of sleeves, grab baskets, and harvest a whole hillside of ripe grapes. I'm deeply grateful to my daughters, Amanda and Melissa, for taking the trip of a lifetime with me and not having a throw-down fit when they saw that starry look in my eyes and knew good and well I was about to go to seed. The loved ones of a writer pay a price. I am immensely thankful for their generosity. Melissa read every single chapter before I turned it in, and her insights, encouragements, questions, and suggestions were solid gold to me. My girls are the chambers of my heart. I cannot imagine doing life of any kind without their love and constant camaraderie.

I so appreciate my husband, Keith, who sees me through every project and in the frenzy of the last hours toward the final deadline, brings me toasted ham and cheese sandwiches with brown mustard, rubs my neck, kisses the top of my frantic head, and says, "Baby, you can do it. God made you for this." He's been more interested in this material than anything I've ever written, and that gift is not wasted on me.

I was so nervous to hear from my literary agents, Sealy and Curtis Yates, after they read the manuscript that I nearly made myself sick. I never know when I turn in a book if it's decent or not. I write on what I find most meaningful in any given season. Such an approach is big on passion, to be sure, but pitifully small on objectivity. To say I was relieved when they responded enthusiastically is an understatement. Throughout the process, I heard from each of them separately about how this or that portion of the book was speaking personally to them. They went way beyond agency. They were true brothers, standing in the open air of a rocky vineyard, digging in that fertile soil with me. I'll never forget it.

I am so grateful to God for Tyndale House Publishers. This is the third project I've had the privilege to work on with them, and they are exceptional people. I have deep respect for Mark Taylor and his long obedience in the same direction. I'm crazy about Maria Eriksen and Andrea Lindgren, and so appreciate their hard work. Ron Beers and Karen Watson are not only partners to me through publishing; they are personal friends and lovers of Scripture and great thinkers. Jan Long Harris worked tirelessly on this project and kept us all on our toes. I owe her a tremendous debt of gratitude and gladly pay it. I had never had the joy of working with Stephanie Rische before. She was recommended to me and turned out to be exactly the right editor for *Chasing Vines*. I'd choose her again for this project one hundred times over. She got the idea from the start.

I interviewed a number of experts in order to broaden my understanding of vines, branches, and vineyards. Each one imparted rich minerals to the soil of research that made this book grow. The first was Gordon Sullivan, a world-renown sommelier and, as God would have it, brother-in-law to a very dear friend of mine. Gordon has as many years invested in grapes as I have invested in Bible study, and I was tickled to find him equally passionate. He was brilliant, fascinating, and utterly delightful. His love for the vine swelled my love for my Vine.

Fred Billings was another expert I interviewed. He is the soil expert, and you can't understand the first thing about how a vine grows if you won't get in the dirt. Keith and I have loved Fred and his wife, Barbie, for decades, and what makes his expertise particularly wonderful is that he sees everything through the lens of a wholehearted Jesus-follower. There were times both of us got tears in our eyes talking about how God makes things grow.

I had the privilege of touring gorgeous vineyards in preparation for this book, deliberately scheduled in different seasons so I could study the vine through the course of the year. My love affair began in a vineyard in Tuscany. It then wooed me west to California wine country, where I first spoke on Isaiah's song of the vineyard. Then I went to the heart-arresting Willamette Valley in Oregon, and finally back to Texas with Paul Vincent and Merrill Bonarrigo, owners of Messina Hof Winery and Resort in Bryan. Lovelier people cannot be found in the full stretch of the Lone Star State. Merrill is a fellow Bible freak and has spoken on numerous occasions about the vine and branches from decades of hands-on experience. She mesmerized me.

Other experts taught me through their books, articles, and podcasts. My copy of Jeff Cox's *From Vines to Wines* is worn nearly to a nub. Tom Powers's *The Organic Backyard Vineyard* and Robert E.

White's *Understanding Vineyard Soils* were greatly helpful. Gisela Kreglinger's *The Spirituality of Wine* and Norman Wirzba's *Food and Faith: A Theology of Eating* were lovely, insightful, and stirring. Robert Farrar Capon's *The Supper of the Lamb* is simply spectacular, and if you're a foodie and it's not somewhere on your shelf, remedy that situation immediately. Alongside countless Bible commentaries and resources, these have been my most prominent teachers in the sublime field of grapes and vines. I loved every minute of research this project demanded.

My heart overflows with gratitude to God for my coworkers at Living Proof Ministries. They are not only my partners in ministry; they are my dearest friends on earth. They cheer me on from the first inkling of a writing project to the fruition of the book on their nightstands. They keep everything else at the ministry going so I can spend most of my time doing research, writing materials, and teaching the Scriptures. I am not worthy of them, but I am deeply grateful to God for them.

I am almost without words to express my thankfulness to God for readers. For people who still love a sizable book in a world of sound bites. For people pushing back against a culture bound and determined to rob us of our God-given attention spans. To my fellow bookworms, who love nothing better than the sound of a book spine breaking—cheers! Here's to taking the time. Here's to feeding our minds. And above all else, here's to chasing the Vine, who turns water into wine.

Jesus, thank You. Your grace has so abounded to me. Oh, let it not be in vain. Take this book and do with it what You will. I wrote every word of it because of You. You are my vine. You are my plate. You are my wine. It is to Your Father's glory that I bear much fruit, showing myself to be Your disciple. So, blessed Savior, Light and Love, see to it.

NOTES

CHAPTER 1: PLANT

1. Walter William Skeat, *A Concise Etymological Dictionary of the English Language* (London: Clarendon Press, 1885), 211.
2. Skeat, 211.

CHAPTER 2: PLACE

1. Robert E. White, *Understanding Vineyard Soils* (Oxford: Oxford University Press, 2009), 25.
2. White, 17.
3. Jeff Cox, *From Vines to Wines: The Complete Guide to Growing Grapes and Making Your Own Wine* (North Adams, MA: Storey, 2015), 6.

CHAPTER 3: GRAPES

1. Will Oremus, "Lies Travel Faster Than Truth on Twitter—and Now We Know Who to Blame," *Slate: Future Tense*, March 9, 2018, https://slate.com/technology /2018/03 /lies-travel-faster-than-truth-on-twitter-says-a-major-new-mit-study.html.
2. Eugene H. Merrill, *Deuteronomy: An Exegetical and Theological Exposition of Holy Scripture*, vol. 4 (Nashville: B & H, 1994), 186.
3. L. H. Bailey in Jeff Cox, *From Vines to Wines: The Complete Guide to Growing Grapes and Making Your Own Wine* (North Adams, MA: Storey, 2015), 14.

CHAPTER 4: SONG

1. John D. W. Watts, *Isaiah 1–33*, vol. 24 (Nashville: Thomas Nelson, 2005), 83.

CHAPTER 6: HILLS

1. Jeff Cox, *From Vines to Wines: The Complete Guide to Growing Grapes and Making Your Own Wine* (North Adams, MA: Storey, 2015), 47.

CHAPTER 7: ROCKS

1. Jeff Cox, *From Vines to Wines: The Complete Guide to Growing Grapes and Making Your Own Wine* (North Adams, MA: Storey, 2015), 43.
2. Cox, 43.

3. Jamie Goode, "Struggling Vines Produce Better Wines," Wineanorak.com, http://www.wineanorak.com/struggle.htm.

4. Goode, http://www.wineanorak.com/struggle.htm.

5. Karen MacNeil, "The Sex Life of Wine Grapes," *WineSpeed* (blog), May 25, 2018, https://winespeed.com/blog/2018/05/the-sex-life-of-wine-grapes/.

CHAPTER 8: VINE

1. For an in-depth look at the first-century Passover table, see Joel B. Green, *The Gospel of Luke* (Grand Rapids, MI: Eerdmans, 1997), 757–58.

2. Walter L. Liefeld, "Luke" in Frank E. Gaebelein, ed., *The Expositor's Bible Commentary: Matthew, Mark, Luke*, vol. 8 (Grand Rapids, MI: Zondervan, 1984), 1026.

3. Gary M. Burge, *The NIV Application Commentary: John* (Grand Rapids, MI: Zondervan, 2000), 416.

4. Burge, 417.

CHAPTER 9: ABIDE

1. *Merriam-Webster's Collegiate Dictionary*, 11th ed. (Springfield, MA: Merriam-Webster, Inc., 2003).

2. Gary M. Burge, *The NIV Application Commentary: John* (Grand Rapids, MI: Zondervan, 2000), 426.

3. Burge, 426.

4. Marvin R. Vincent, *Word Studies in the New Testament*, vol. 2 (New York: Scribner, 1887), 249.

CHAPTER 10: PRUNING

1. Jeff Cox, *From Vines to Wines: The Complete Guide to Growing Grapes and Making Your Own Wine* (North Adams, MA: Storey, 2015), 79.

2. Cox, 75.

CHAPTER 11: TRELLIS

1. Jeff Cox, *From Vines to Wines: The Complete Guide to Growing Grapes and Making Your Own Wine* (North Adams, MA: Storey, 2015), viii.

CHAPTER 12: SOIL

1. Andrew Jefford, foreword to Robert E. White, *Understanding Vineyard Soils* (Oxford: Oxford University Press, 2015), vii.

2. Jeff Cox, *From Vines to Wines: The Complete Guide to Growing Grapes and Making Your Own Wine* (North Adams, MA: Storey, 2015), 45.

3. Robert E. White, *Understanding Vineyard Soils*, (Oxford: Oxford University Press, 2015), 5.

4. White, 183.

5. White, 175.

CHAPTER 13: ROOTS

1. See Deuteronomy 5:15; 7:18; 8:1; 32:7; Joshua 1:13; Nehemiah 4:14; Psalm 105:5-6.

CHAPTER 14: ALFRESCO

1. Wendell Berry, *The Art of the Commonplace: The Agrarian Essays of Wendell Berry (Berkeley, CA: Counterpoint, 2002)*, 311. Thanks to Gisela H. Kreglinger, who made this connection in *The Spirituality of Wine* (Grand Rapids, MI: Eerdmans, 2016).
2. 1 Kings 17–18.

CHAPTER 15: MANURE

1. John Nolland, *Luke 9:21–18:34*, vol. 35B (Dallas: Word, 1998), 719.
2. Joel B. Green, *The Gospel of Luke* (Grand Rapids, MI: Eerdmans, 1997), 515.

CHAPTER 16: PESTILENCE

1. Parts of this chapter originally appeared in Beth Moore, "To Servants of Jesus in Your 30s and 40s," *The LMP Blog*, May 23, 2016, https://blog.lproof.org/2016/05/to-servants-of-jesus-in-your-30s-and-40s.html.

CHAPTER 17: INGATHERING

1. Chad Brand et al., eds., "Festivals," in *Holman Illustrated Bible Dictionary* (Nashville: Holman Bible, 2003), 569.
2. Ralph Gower, *The New Manners and Customs of Bible Times* (Chicago: Moody Press, 1987), 106.
3. Leon Morris, *The Gospel according to John* (Grand Rapids, MI: Eerdmans, 1995), 598.
4. R. H. Strachan, *The Fourth Gospel* (London: Student Christian Movement Press, 1955), quoted in Leon Morris, *The Gospel according to John* (Grand Rapids, MI: Eerdmans, 1995), 598.

CHAPTER 18: GLEANINGS

1. Joel B. Green, *The Gospel of Luke*, (Grand Rapids, MI: Eerdmans, 1997), 430.

CHAPTER 19: FEAST

1. Robert Farrar Capon, *The Supper of the Lamb* (New York: Farrar, Straus and Giroux, 1989), 84.

ABOUT THE AUTHOR

Author and speaker Beth Moore is a dynamic teacher whose conferences take her across the globe. Beth founded Living Proof Ministries in 1994 with the purpose of encouraging women to know and love Jesus through the study of Scripture. She has written numerous bestselling books and Bible studies, including *Breaking Free, Believing God, Entrusted,* and *The Quest,* which have been read by women of all ages, races, and denominations. Another recent addition includes her first work of fiction, *The Undoing of Saint Silvanus.*

Beth recently celebrated twenty years of Living Proof Live conferences. She can be seen teaching Bible studies on the television program *Living Proof with Beth Moore,* aired on the Trinity Broadcasting Network.

She and her husband of forty years reside in Houston, Texas. She is a dedicated wife, the mother of two adult daughters, and the grandmother of three delightful grandchildren.

Join Beth on her journey of discovering what it means to chase vines.

Learn to fully embrace God's amazing design for a fruitful, abundant, and meaningful life.

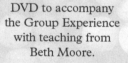

Great for small group or individual Bible study.

DVD to accompany the Group Experience with teaching from Beth Moore.

Join Beth Moore on a fruitful journey through thirty-one unforgettable promises from God's Word.

CP1548

Chronic insecurity is becoming a cultural epidemic, and it's time we did something about it. It's time to say, "So long!" to insecurity. Join trusted Bible teacher Beth Moore on a quest for real, lasting, soul-deep security.

So Long, Insecurity: Women of all ages and backgrounds will resonate with Beth's message of security and discover truths that will free them emotionally and spiritually and lead them to a better life as they walk with God.

So Long, Insecurity Group Experience (leader's guide also available): An important tool for small groups, Bible studies, and book clubs, the *So Long, Insecurity Group Experience* takes readers on a journey deep into God's Word and encourages them to work through their struggles with insecurity together while growing in knowledge of the only One who can provide lasting security.

So Long, Insecurity Devotional Journal: The truths in *So Long, Insecurity* get even more personal with this beautiful devotional journal, which includes Scripture, prayers, and guided questions to help readers record their own journeys toward soul-deep security.

The Promise of Security: This 64-page booklet provides a portable boost of hope and confidence that will encourage women on their quest for true security.

Available online and at a bookstore near you! If you'd like to symbolically "send off" your insecurity, go to www.solonginsecurity.com.　CP0473

MORE FROM BETH MOORE

BIBLE STUDIES

- *A Woman's Heart: God's Dwelling Place*
- *David: A Heart like His*
- *To Live Is Christ*
- *Living Beyond Yourself: Exploring the Fruit of the Spirit*
- *Breaking Free*
- *Beloved Disciple*
- *Believing God*
- *The Patriarchs*
- *Daniel*
- *Living Free*
- *Stepping Up: A Journey through the Psalms of Ascent*
- *Esther: It's Tough to Be a Woman*
- *James: Mercy Triumphs*
- *Sacred Secrets*
- *Children of the Day*
- *Entrusted*
- *The Quest*

NONFICTION

- *Audacious*
- *Believing God*
- *So Long, Insecurity*
- *Get Out of That Pit*
- *Feathers from My Nest*
- *When Godly People Do Ungodly Things*

- *My Child My Princess*
- *Whispers of Hope*
- *Praying God's Word*
- *Things Pondered*
- *A Quick Word with Beth Moore*
- *Believing God Day by Day*
- *Believing God Devotional Journal*
- *Breaking Free Day by Day*
- *Delivered*
- *Further Still*
- *Jesus, the One and Only*
- *Looking Up*
- *Looking Up Devotional Journal*
- *Portraits of Devotion*
- *Praying God's Word Day by Day*

FICTION

- *The Undoing of Saint Silvanus*

DVD TEACHINGS

- *Wising Up Wherever Life Happens*
- *The Inheritance*
- *Here and Now, There and Then*
- *The Law of Love*
- *Breath: The Life of God in Us*

FOR INFORMATION ABOUT LIVING PROOF WITH BETH MOORE,
✦ VISIT BETHMOORE.ORG. ✦   CP1120